D0891844

BIRD HUNTING TACTICS

Proven game-getting techniques
and sound, down-to-earth advice
on all aspects of upland bird hunting.

By DAVID MICHAEL DUFFEY

FOR BECKY JEAN DUFFEY,
just for being my granddaughter
... and for the many men, women and dogs,
both good and bad, who have been mentors,
companions, diversions, challenges and were
influential in sparing me life's hardest knocks.

BIRD HUNTING TACTICS
Second Edition

Illustrated by Rockne Knuth.

"Bird Hunting Tactics" was originally published in 1968
under the title, "Bird Hunting Know-How," by D. Van Nostrand, Inc.

First edition, "Bird Hunting Tactics," published by Willow
Creek Press, Oshkosh, Wisconsin.

PRINTED IN THE UNITED STATES OF AMERICA

ISBN - 0-932558-52-6

Table of Contents

Introduction

MANY sportsmen are fanatics. The waterfowler delves exhaustively into the best way to lay out a string of diver decoys and may even start carving his own; the whitetailed-deer hunter can argue for hours about the pros and cons of telescopic sights, and so on into the night.

But if these men are nuts, they can't hold a candle to the man who calls himself an upland bird hunter when it comes to devotion to a favorite hunting sport and both autumnal and off-season eccentricities.

Not only is upland game bird hunting one of the most democratic of all the hunting sports, it is more generalized, offers a great variety of activity and is the subject of more sage advice, personal opinion and hot air regarding how to get the most out of a day in the field than any other form of hunting.

The chances are that you are reading this book either because you already hunt upland game (or plan to) and want to know more about it, or because you figure you know just about all there is to know about at least some phase of this sport, and you want to see what kind of rash statements some armchair writer has made in regard to your favorite bird, gun or dog.

So whether you want to learn something new or just enjoy an open season on authors, please be my guest.

Upland bird hunting is, as stated above, a widely varied and truly democratic sport. You'll find partridge and quail pursued by country boys in bib-overalls and barn boots out on the back forty, as well as by custom-tailored scions of wealth and power who have hunted the world over. In between, there are a lot of hunters (like me) who don't *quite* fit either description, and it's possible or even probable that all these experiences won't dovetail.

So let me clear the air at the outset—I *don't* know everything there is to know about hunting ruffed grouse, woodcock, pheasant, bobwhite, sharptails, prairie chicken, Hungarian partridge or chukar. (And I'm not even going to mention some of the more esoteric upland game birds about which I know almost nothing.) As a matter of fact, I hope to go on learning more about upland game birds until the day I die, a day which I sincerely hope will not be too far removed from the memory of an unexpected flush in heavy cover, the feel of a favorite shotgun as it comes up, the expression of a bird dog who knows he's done right and the special fever that hits you when the hunting season opens.

But even if I don't profess to know everything there is to know, it won't hurt you to be polite and humor me. I may have accidentally stumbled across something you missed, or perhaps my different experience has taught me something that would be useful for you to know.

For whatever its faults, this book is based on practical, first-hand experience. Don't expect to find a lot of paper research based on the learned studies of professional academicians, but don't look, either, for a distillation of ancient hunting lore handed down orally from daddy and his daddy's daddy before him—because if that's what you want, I'm going to disappoint you.

Don't get me wrong. I don't mean to disparage the things we can learn from *anybody* who has a lot of experience with game birds. There may not be many biologists who are crack wing shots, but that's no reason to belittle their research and carefully compiled statistics. And whether you like it or not, they're going to continue to have a lot to say about how long the hunting season runs and what the bag limit is.

At the other extreme, the senior resident "old timer" may be talking through his battered hat about the cause and effect of game cycles, but you'd be out of your cotton-pickin' mind to turn down his invitation to show you where the birds are.

What I've mostly tried to do in this book, however, is to tell you what I've learned from my experience, rather than rehashing what some other guy learned from his. And when it comes to bird hunting, I've been a lucky guy, for as a free-lance outdoor writer, the outdoor editor of a metropolitan newspaper, hunting dogs editor of *OUTDOOR LIFE* magazine for 23 years and currently contributing regularly to a handful of national publications like Petersen's *HUNTING, GUN DOG, WING & SHOT* and *HUNTING RETRIEVER*, a part-time game warden and guide, I've had more than my share of opportunities to hunt game birds.

Yes, I've been lucky and then some, because at heart I'm a hunter, not a writer, and anyone who can scrape a living out of doing what he loves doesn't have much to complain about. So this, then, is a book *for* hunters, *by* a hunter.

Why is it that hunting means so much to me?

I can't say, for sure. It's not that I need the meat, or enjoy counting coup on a record number of birds. And I sure don't get mystical about the game birds I pursue—I ventilate them every chance I get, secure in the belief that the odds are with the bird.

Possibly the main reason I keep coming back for more is that never, while hunting upland game, have I wanted to be in any other place or at any other time. Hunting absorbs a man with the right now, leaving no room for past regrets or future anxieties. If it's not like this for you—well, I hope you're luckier in some other way. But if you're like me, read on while I try to show you where the birds are and tell you how to get the most enjoyment out of bagging them. Now let's get started!

1

Upland Superbird
THE RUFFED GROUSE

DEDICATED bird hunters have been known to have nightmares about ruffed grouse. Some of these devotees, after intensive research into the life and loves of *Bonasa umbellus,* have sublimated their anxieties by producing erudite articles or fanciful stories about this timber-edge bomber. For such hunters, the ruffed grouse has become more than a mere game bird, more than a symbol; it's Superbird!

On the other hand, many of the semi-literate folk who live around the out-of-the-way places which ruffed grouse prefer tend to view this particular bird in a very different light. To such backwoodsmen, a "partridge" (often pronounced "pottage") is meat on the table—the chicken of the woods—it's just a dumb bird, easily butchered.

Now the attitudes and ideas of most upland bird hunters about ruffed grouse and how to hunt them usually derive from one or the other of those extremes. To the sporting gentleman who spends more dollars on the latest in outdoor garb than he spends minutes in the woods, a ruffed grouse is something to be discussed in reverent tones. A hunt is considered a success if two or three birds are even *seen.* Just *hearing* a wily bird lift from the other side of a screen of cover can be the day's high point.

With only an occasional gulp, this follower of the sport swallows virtually everything either game management officials or outdoor writers have to say about bird populations, and where and how birds should be hunted. Accordingly, when the birds are at the bottom of their periodic cycles his dog is at fault for not finding more. When the partridge are popping out on every tote road he'll cuss a newly acquired gun, the shells, maybe even himself when he misses a bird on the wing. He'll listen to most suggestions, for he is seeking a bird-producing formula of his own.

But should you be introduced to ruffed-grouse shooting by a professional "old timer" (or even a semi-pro), there will be little reverence in his attitude toward game. And he is well-nigh incurable, for partridge are easy to pot shoot.

Birds are to be taken any way possible—this is the creed of the "old timer" and his proteges. Conversation about hunting among these people does not revolve around the sight and sound of game. It is centered on how many bag limits were filled out in a day.

This type of hunter is happy and hunts only when the partridge populations are up. When they are down, he gripes long and loud about the stupidities of the two-legged jackasses in the conservation department and the cleverness of the predators and winged raptors competing with him for their share of the bird crop.

Time spent afield when the birds are down is wasted time, just as shooting at flying birds is a waste of shells. There is no telling such a hunter anything! For he is convinced that the gospel according to Mose Bosely, Lafe Turner, or some other bewhiskered connoisseur of rough-cut plug, is the final word on the subject.

So any attempt at practical writing on ruffed-grouse hunting will run head on into putting to rest the fanciful dreams and nightmares of one element and overcoming the stubborn prejudices of another. But let's try.

In the north country, the ruffed grouse and its odd-looking little sidekick, the woodcock, remain about the last challenge for the hunter who would rather gun a true sporting bird than eat, sleep or make love. Since it ranks as one of the larger upland game birds, there are times when the neophyte (or even the expert, in dense cover) will at least momentarily confuse a ruffed grouse with a hen pheasant, a sharp-tailed grouse or a prairie chicken. In various parts of the nation the range and habitat of these birds overlap.

The name ruffed grouse probably stems from the neck ruff of the bird that can be raised and lowered like an umbrella. This probably also contributed to the bird's Latin name. Adult grouse may reach almost two pounds in weight and are about 18 inches long. Males are slightly larger than females. The cock's tail is usually longer than the hen's, and the ruff longer and showing more of a metallic sheen. But the surest means of field identification, once a bird is in the bag, involves the color band at the end of the cock's tail—it is unbroken across the entire width. The band on the hen's tail, particularly on the underside, is broken in the two center feathers, as a rule. There is no sure means of differentiating between the sexes when they are in flight.

Ruffed grouse show some general color variations. Probably the majority are gray or at least grayish brown. Some are brown, others rufous or almost red.

Including its various sub-species, the ruffed grouse is fairly well distributed through Canada and the United States, except for the deep South and Southwest. It is most popular among hunters in the New England and upper-Midwestern states.

GROUSE-HUNTING TACTICS

"Where are the birds?"

Anyone who has guided or been guided on a bird hunting trip knows that after the initial pleasantries are exchanged this question, or a variation thereof, is the first thing asked.

Hunters may not realize it, but they are concerned with ruffed grouse *habitat* more than anything else. For if there is any pattern to bird behavior it is dictated to a great extent by the food and cover available. Where a partridge feeds, where he seeks refuge and where he's likely to be *during the hunting season* must be known by the hunter. If a hunter cannot locate good country and birds, to what avail is his fancy firearm or his pedigreed pup?

The story about a partridge's life and what he does is interesting, even during that *other* part of the year real hunters would prefer not to think about, the closed season. This is great stuff for bird watchers and many books have been written about ruffed grouse by bird watchers. But it won't help a hunter much except for one thing. It'll teach him that where the birds are in the spring, summer and winter ain't necessarily where they'll be in the fall, when it's legal to shoot them.

So I'm not going to waste your time now with a detailed description of what a ruffed grouse looks like, when and how he mates, how he manages to survive the winter and such like. Read about it sometime when you can't get out hunting. Skip it and you won't hurt my feelings, and it won't hurt your bird hunting, either.

If you get into an argument about partridge and want to quote a widely traveled authority, leave me out. My ruffed-grouse hunting has been confined largely to Wisconsin and the upper peninsula of Michigan. Why travel for something you have in your backyard? I mean this literally. I do use an automobile frequently to reach some hunting spot. But I don't have to. I can walk out my back door with a shotgun, take a couple dogs out of the kennel and start my hunt on foot from there.

Virtually daily hunting during the open season, and the conviction that game birds behave pretty much the same, regardless of where they are hatched, have given me the temerity to write this book. I don't expect that what I say will go without challenge. You may very well run into situations in your favorite hunting country that don't quite jibe with what I've discovered.

In examining my credentials please give consideration to the fact that my home state has many and widely varied grouse grounds, including the Ozark-like bluff country in the west, the river floods plains with their blow sand ridges in the central part of the state, and the timbered lake country of the far north. I hope one of these is comparable to the country you know, for a ruffed-grouse hunter develops an insatiable fondness for the familiarity of his own grounds.

So much for the generalities. Let's get to specifics. Ruffed grouse, alias partridge, pats, birds or even "that-s.o.b.-that-got-away" are where you find them. Often this will be in rough country, those wild and the semi-wild lands that enrich lumbermen and impoverish farmers. Yet, it is a mistake to call grouse uncivilized. Of all our native game, partridge have managed to survive in some of the most highly developed areas in the country, holding out in seemingly insignificant little pockets of rough country. It is probably for this reason that they have been ac-

14

corded inordinate respect from sportsmen in our crowded Eastern states.

Fundamentally, however, they are backwoods birds, found in their greatest numbers in areas that suffer only infrequently from human incursions. Survival has occurred without the aid of the elaborate management schemes by which conservation agencies have attempted to preserve and promulgate other upland game game species, foreign and domestic.

"Ruffed grouse," say some wildlife experts, "are impossible to manage." Hunters can only hope this is true. For the fear is that when the key is found to open the door to a flood of ruffed-grouse research and management programs, this wonderful bird may become so well managed he'll cease to exist in huntable numbers.

In the fifty years I've known him intimately, despite periodic ups and downs and the increase in hunter numbers, he's held his own since the late years of the Great Depression, the bag limit in Wisconsin has been fairly constant. It was four a day and eight in possession in the early 1940s. When birds were up in the 1950s, limits of five and ten were established and have prevailed into the 1990s except for reductions to three and five with a down cycle of birds in the '60s. Open seasons almost state-wide over four *months* in length have been in vogue, in both good and bad times (contrasting with World War II era seasons continuous in some areas for only three *weeks* with split seasons in others measured in terms of days) starting in September and ending in January.

Much emphasis has been placed by some writers on a hunter's ability to recognize certain brush and shrub species and to know the fruit, nuts, buds and other forage partridge prefer. This is excellent knowledge to possess. It can also provide a sideline hobby to go with your hunting. But I'm not a botanist and I assume that you aren't either. We're hunters. Our knowledge of things botanical will be limited by the time we have to devote to its study. Overdoing it will detract from hunting time.

So, while I dutifully examine the crop contents of each partridge I shoot, it may well be that I can't identify by proper name more than a few of the items found there: acorns, beechnuts, catkins, buds, greens, berries, seeds and even corn kernels. (Ah yes, despite disclaimers, ruffed grouse will feed on grains if available).

These observations don't greatly influence my hunting strategy. Ruffed grouse can make out on a variety of food and do. They take what's available. Besides, reading bird crops can lead you astray. That bird with a crop full of clover you killed in the morning might have sought something more substantial by afternoon, had he not been killed. He might have given you a crop bursting with acorns had he been flushed and dropped just before closing time. All a crop exam really tells you is that the bird has been feeding.

In other words, while recognizing the items in a bird's crop and being able to match them with what's on the ground and on the bushes can be an *aid* in ruffed-grouse hunting, it is by no means the key to success. To contribute substantially to hunting success, the food and feeding must be correlated with the weather, the time of day and the hunting method the man prefers.

But you can't wait to learn "the secret to successful partridge hunting"? Okay! You may not like it; it requires few brains and less education. But here it is: All you need is ambition, curiosity and a good pair of legs. Yup! that form of locomotion threatened with extinction in the U.S.—walking—is the secret.

To make this system unbeatable, walk behind a hunting dog. You have a wide choice (as is indicated in another chapter) and what kind is up to you. But a poor dog will show you more birds than you'll see alone. A good one will educate you.

"We're on our way, old buddy," said the cheery voice on the other end of the line. "We're packed and pullin' out in an hour."

"What in hell are you talking about?" I asked. "You woke me up from a sound sleep." I'm not good at voices on the phone any time of the day or night, and it was some past my 8 to 10 P.M. retiring time during the hunting season.

"This is By. Pat's right here. We got jammed up. But we're hot to trot now. Remember? You said you'd take us bird hunting tomorrow."

I did remember then. But when I made the date I'd neglected

to scratch it on my calendar. By was an ad salesman working out of the Chicago office of *OUTDOOR LIFE* magazine, for which I wrote a monthly dog column and Pat was a fellow free-lance writer. Both lived in Northbrook, a Chicago suburb.

When I answered, it wasn't for the purpose of discouraging them, although it may have sounded that way. I was just trying to outline the situation as honestly as possible.

It was late in the season. Pheasant hunting is marginal where I live, mostly stocked birds. Waterfowl hunting had been poor, but we'd give it a quick riffle with an early morning jump shoot on some potholes. That would leave ruffed grouse and woodcock. But I sure wouldn't guarantee anything. The grouse population had struck me as being only fair in the early weeks and now, by the second week in November, they'd been pretty well shot over. The bulk of the woodcock flight, always my ace in the hole, had passed through. Besides, there was some weather moving in.

But that summation didn't discourage Byron Warnes and Patrick Snook any more than my warning that we'd probably have to do a lot of hiking. They didn't care what. They hadn't had any wild gunning, they had their licenses and they wanted to shoot. They pulled into my yard at 4 A.M., bringing rain, sleet and a bottle of bourbon with them. I had one drink with them, then crawled back into bed.

When I lit the fire under the coffee at 5:30, By was curled up in front of the coals in the fireplace and Pat was sprawled on the sofa. I woke them at 6 A.M. We had only five miles to drive and I had the dogs loaded.

We hit the pothole country between 6:30 and 7 A.M., and it was wet. The pair of Labradors and I plunged down into the timbered marsh spit to see if we could move some ducks, while Pat and By deployed as flankers along the edge, slogging through the high wet grass. The ducks weren't in and hadn't been, if the absence of feathers on the water was any indication. We saw one mallard in the air before going back to the four-wheel-drive Scout, where I peeled off my waders and put on walking boots.

There was a good "walking road," a rutted path through a swamp that is three miles long and always produces a bird or two at least, plus a forty-acre piece that is another sure bet. But we went birdless. They weren't out on the road and the bulk of the forty acres was under instep-high water. Needless to say, by the time we wound up that hike I was as wet as the other two. We stopped in town long enough to wolf down a brunch, then hit another choice piece of cover. There we saw our first birds and downed a brace of fat woodcock and one ruffed grouse.

Although I apologized for the slowness of the hunt, Pat and By would have none of it, actually expressing pleasure over the size of what were presumably large flight woodcock. But it irked me because three prior visits to that cover had produced a sum total of sixteen ruffed grouse and eighty-six woodcock flushes. I had my best upland bird dogs down, Flirt, an English Springer bitch, and Poncho, a Labrador who is trained to hunt in the manner of a spaniel.

Just for a change, we left the miserable dripping brush and got into some more open country on a deserted public hunting area. I put down two pointing dogs. They coursed over the big marsh and highlands and pointed two hen pheasants. Only cocks are legal.

It was getting late in the afternoon and a fog was closing things up. "We got one more place to go," I announced. Never was I more impressed by the willingness of two sportsmen to work for their game. I knew they were bushed. I do this sort of thing every day, but I was feeling it by that time too. Wading through twenty miles of wet cover with waterfilled boots is no picnic.

But that "one more place" paid off. We found birds on the brush edge of a little logged-off island in the middle of a marsh. Even though quitting time still was a few minutes off it was hard to see to shoot. The fog had gotten so thick I was lucky to find the Scout, although we were never more than three forties from the parked vehicle. But we were three happy hunters. We'd wound up with shooting at ten ruffed grouse and seventeen woodcock, most of it within the last hour of shooting. That does make a man forget the uncomfortable, frustrating hours that preceded it.

This hunting experience is cited for a number of reasons, but chiefly to illustrate what I meant when I said hunting success or lack of it is more involved than just knowing what bird country looks like or where food is available. Every piece of cover we were in was proven good bird habitat.

But the weather was abominable. In a cold, wet rain birds sit tight. This, in itself, makes it hard for dogs to find them, for inactive birds don't give off much scent. Maybe things picked up just before quitting time because hungry birds moved to feed despite the weather. The fog, apparently rising from the "warm" ground into the chill evening air, may also have contributed better scenting conditions.

But it should bring home my major thesis. If you are willing to work for your birds you'll be virtually sure to get some shooting. A determined willingness to traverse good grouse cover until you finally locate birds is the key to successful hunting. If you've found a better way to do it, my hat's off to you. Me, maybe I'm just too dumb to do anything but walk and keep walking until the dogs get into them.

So, don't get up on your high horse. A Southern plantation quail hunter you ain't. A Northern ruffed-grouse hunter you are. Instead, pull on your boots, the most comfortable you have. We're now ready to take a hike through some good grouse cover.

Someday, if someone were to offer me a bit of Heaven, I'd settle for the following description:

Just give me a section of land, laced with scrub oak, aspen- and birch-covered sand ridges, containing a small lake or two with a marshy shoreline, a few scattered stands of hardwood on a rocky ridge with an undergrowth of raspberry brush and wild grape vines, some scattered plots of cleared land and maybe a small abandoned orchard, an alternately wet and dry bog with some cranberries or blueberries, a cedar swamp with scattered conifers around it and a meandering stream with a few spring creeks feeding it, the tag alder, red osier and willow brush thick along their banks.

That describes one heavenly place to hunt ruffed grouse. You can bet that as a bonus you'd have woodcock shooting and you'd be sure of a crack at deer. The same country that deer find delectable is also good grouse country, and woodcock frequently share good lowland grouse coverts. Fortunately, grouse don't need a heaven to exist. Any one of the types of cover described could be a grouse haven.

If you've hunted much, you almost unconsciously come to recognize birdy spots, not just because such and such a species of something or other grows there but from a combination of things. In that type of setting, at that time of day, in that kind of weather you have found birds in such a place. I will try to describe likely cover. But there's only one way you'll develop a sixth sense for it. That's by hunting on foot.

Yes, you can learn without the aid of a dog. But it will take you longer.

Don't be surprised to find yourself rocked back on your heels when a grouse rockets up from some unexpected place. They can be found almost anywhere in wild country. I wouldn't waste time hunting tilled fields, open pastures, solid mature pine stands, clean forest floor hardwood stands, expanses of open marsh or a street in downtown Chicago. But except for the Illinois metropolis, I'd certainly be on the alert when skirting the *edges* of the aforementioned "dead areas."

Like much of our other game, ruffed grouse are birds of the edge. You might well find a single bird, a pair or, early in the season, a covey in the brush along the edge of a cornfield; in a clump of aspen or birch in a cow pasture; in any opening in big timber; around deserted farm buildings or logging operations; or on an island of brush and trees in the middle of a swamp or marsh.

Cutover country, if you can find it anymore what with reforestation, is an excellent grouse-hunting bet, especially when the succession of aspen and basswood is just getting underway. Sloppily logged hardwood stands with plenty of tops and slash lying around should produce. Any place having an emergent growth of mixed conifer and hardwood is likely to provide the grouse hunter with sport.

Grouse cover can range from sublime to ridiculous. Classic grouse cover would have plenty of thickets but the cover would be well broken. Birch and aspen would be in clumps and islands, or small stands at the most. Creek bottoms would be brush covered, but not impenetrable jungles or too extensive. Brushy potholes and draws, dry or wet depending upon the weather, should be no larger than half a city block, or else long and narrow. Sand path

roads, stone fences that can be climbed over, berry brush and thorns that can be skirted rather than bulled through.

Classic grouse cover is a wonderful place to shoot and to take pictures when the birds are in it. It's open enough so a diligent, good-moving pointing dog can be kept track of. A man can set himself for shots over a dog on point. He can swing his gun unimpeded and the bird may well cross an open spot to get to another clump of cover. Oh! If it could always be like that! But would it be grouse hunting? I doubt it.

Chances are good you are going to find your birds in some kind of cover that borders on the ridiculous, rather than a bobwhite quail venue in the miniature. No recreation seeker in his right mind would venture into this stuff. But the devoted partridge pusher, driven by the frustration of hearing more birds than he's seen, having blown three easy chances and then scored an impossible, *is not in his right mind*. Such a hunter will penetrate anything that promises to hold birds or screens them from him.

Let's not get the wrong idea. I for one don't go along with a theory advanced by game managers every time the ruffed grouse population drops. "Hunters just aren't getting back in the brush," the experts wail. "That's why they aren't seeing any birds." Maybe there is some explainable reason for those claims. Maybe it's an effort to con the uninitiated. But whatever the reason, that conclusion is wetter than a lumberjack's dream.

I hunt the brush. But I also hunt the logging roads—during the week, when a man stands a fighting chance of dodging an occasional jeep. On weekends the traffic flow is just too heavy. So I don't hunt the brush country because there are more birds there. It's to get away from vehicle-borne "road hunters."

I walk through a lot of brush country and even big timber. I'm on my way to some clearing or some trail that's impassable for vehicles. The birds prefer edge and openings, and the old tote roads with their greens, grit and sunshine gravy are irresistible to ruffed grouse. Even when vehicular traffic makes overgrown logging roads untenable for birds, dogs or men, if one does not find birds within gunshot of these forest avenues early in the morning and late in the afternoon, the bird population is in pretty sorry shape.

So I get the hell away from the much-traveled roads because

I don't like the competition, because I prefer solitude and because walking makes me feel right about hunting. Besides, at midday, the heavy stuff is where the birds go and I like to make a day of it whenever possible. If I never see another hunter the entire day, and this happens frequently, my day is better for it. So this attitude has led to the discovery of many ridiculous hunting strips. Should your preferences parallel mine, I recommend them to you. Otherwise the old road edges, even some lightly traveled country and town "highways" are your byway to the best places to find ruffed grouse.

Be especially alert at trail intersections, where there are triangles of thick cover. If the tote road leads to a young pine plantation, if it is hemmed in with popple and birch or has any kind of food, sumac, wintergreen, berries or grapes nearby, work it over. In the thick cover or when walking a road, utilize a flushing rather than a pointing dog. He'll produce you the world's sportiest shooting and recover what you knock down.

When "walking up" ruffed grouse, with or without a dog, go slow and easy, stopping often. The walk-and-stop technique will put birds in the air that you'd walk past if you kept a steady pace. You worry a bird into the air when you pause for a while. A constant noise reassures a bird, for he knows where you are and what you are doing has not hurt him. But he'll get jittery if he cannot locate you.

That's why you'll hear hunters so often cussing the perversity through which ruffed grouse always seem to flush when the hunter is in an awkward, can't-shoot, position, such as climbing through a fence or blowing his nose. But it's the break in the walking pattern, not the bird's intelligence that puts him to flight.

As a practical matter, this is also why dogs of the pointing breeds usually have so much trouble handling ruffed grouse properly. Just as (or right after) the dog slams down on point—when most birds sit tight—the ruffed grouse gets up, before the hunter can come up for an easy shot. It's the sudden break in tempo and noise that spooks him.

Your toughest shooting will come in the ridiculous cover. From the outside it may look like a solid block of brush or a dreary stand of mixed popple, birch, oak, cedar and spruce. Investigation will reveal islands and clearings inside that harbor birds. Difficulties involve getting to the birds and hitting them in this stuff. You may actually shoot birds from the hip as you fight through a tangle.

Another cover type that will pay off but takes work to reach are the "popple islands" out in the grass marshes. These small landmarks, usually with trees and brushy edge, hold a lot of birds. But often a wet marsh must be waded to reach them. Points of dry land jutting out into the marsh are also excellent spots.

Two types of cover I particularly like to hunt which aren't too rough, as a rule, are the edge between a ridge and a swamp or along a creek bottom. Usually the cover strip along a creek is not too wide and if the cover isn't too thick you can work through it. If it's dense with boggy footing and you have a spaniel or retriever, send the dog down into the thick stuff and stay out along the edge. Shoot your birds when they break out or top the cover. If there is an oak, popple or birch ridge sloping down to a marsh or creek you'll be sure to find birds on either the slope or the brushy edge. There'll be plenty of cover for a bird to dodge behind, but you can usually swing a gun freely.

That's what you look for in the line of grouse cover. So let's move into a discussion of that tool you're going to bang away at those birds with—your shotgun and the fodder you stuff it with.

GROUSE GUNS AND LOADS

Perhaps it's futile to try to tell another man what kind of a shotgun he should carry for grouse gunning, or to speculate on what load will best bring down one of those gray-brown bombers of the uplands. Almost everyone who's ever grassed a bird has some pretty definite opinions about what he wants in a gun and load, or has already saddled himself with a misfit he can't afford to get rid of.

Then too, the savvy shooter recognizes that he doesn't get in as much shooting as he'd like. He's had to work to get accustomed to just one gun, but now he knows it, feels best shooting it and would "rather fight than switch." I'm all for that line of thinking, particularly in grouse and woodcock shooting, for if the mounting and firing of your shotgun are not almost conditioned reflexes, the chances are you won't even pop a primer when the partridge goes out. There's no time to think.

If shotgun and load recommendations are purely academic as far as you are concerned, then skip this section. But most of the casual partridge hunters I've run across have just one holy terror of a time hitting birds. I know some who won't even hunt ruffed grouse and woodcock because they've developed such a defeatist attitude. Sure, a certain number of them couldn't hit a barn door if somebody started to slide it open because they can't swing a gun properly on a moving target. But for many others, the fault actually lies in the gun or the load they're using. And believe me, a partridge doesn't need any extra advantage!

About four-fifths of the sportsmen who venture out for ruffed grouse or woodcock are *over-gunned* and *over-loaded*. If you fall in that category, but still hit your share of birds, don't change a thing—I don't want to be blamed for throwing dust in your shooting eye.

However, if you are an *honest* man, one who is more surprised and elated on those occasions when a bird drops than you are dejected when the little rascal keeps going, read on. Maybe I can help you improve your percentage enough to save you from shooting your way into the poorhouse. For the cost of missing in the grouse woods can run to considerable jack, not to mention the time and effort.

In general, what you want for grouse is a light, short-barreled gun with open boring, one that's easy to carry, quick to mount and squirts a well-dispersed charge of shot out the end. Stick with some tightly-choked, long-barreled duck gun, designed for deliberate swinging and soaking up maximum-load recoil—you'll be old and profane before your time if you tote it on grouse hunts. (If it's the only gun you own, do yourself and your bankroll a favor; stuff it with brush loads.)

Any trap or skeet load, as opposed to high-base ammo, will do an adequate job on ruffed grouse. They flush up close. It doesn't take much shot to drop them. *Hitting them is the problem.* Since you are going to be touching off more shots at under thirty yards than over, why a full choke and heavy loads?

Even though light loads are cheaper, you can be sure that a closely inspected shell goes into each box of target loads. Clay-bird shooters are fussy about their ammo's performance and demand proper ballistic balance between powder charge and shot load; most hunters are content if a shell makes a loud bang. Uniformity of shot pattern is more important than high velocity when shooting light-boned upland birds.

If you're skeptical, check it out with your nearest friendly ballistician. He can give you a really scholarly dissertation and provide statistics, graphs and figures. But it will come out pretty much like I've been trying to tell you. When you accept this, you've taken a big step toward better grouse shooting.

This applies particularly to 12-gauge shooters, which most shotgunners are. However, ruffed-grouse shooting is one place where the smaller bores can really shine. If you are using a "little gun" and have enough reservations about light loads to destroy your confidence when you poke at a bird, go ahead and spend your money on super-duper loads. But you don't have to.

What size shot? Nearly forgot that, and maybe we should. More nonsense is bandied about concerning proper size shot than virtually anything in the shooting game. If you center your pattern on a winged target, you'll kill it regardless of whether you're shooting coarse or fine shot.

I've dropped partridge with everything from No. 4 to No. 9 shot. Admittedly, those are the outside sizes; 4's are really too heavy, and 9's too light. But let's not quibble. If you ground-swat birds (discussed in the chapter on hunting methods) maybe 4's are a good thing. If you figure to see a lot of woodcock, a charge of No. 9 is deadly and it will deal effectively with most partridge.

The best load I ever shot was something called a "pigeon load." It was an ounce and a quarter of No. 7 shot pushed by three and a quarter drams equivalent of powder. This really killed 'em dead, pheasants and ducks too, and looked beautiful on a pattern sheet. (Sad to relate, I also managed to miss, even with these paragons.) They don't load 7's any more, but this charge and shot load is still available in No. 7½ and No. 8 shot sizes, the two I consider best for grouse banging. There's not enough difference between No. 7½ and No. 8 to argue about. Early in the year, with the foliage heavy or in country where you might jump a duck or a pheasant, you may want to lean to 7½ or even 6 in high-velocity loads.

Just for the record, a No. 6 pellet will hit harder than a No. 8 because it is heavier. But you can expect a more dense pattern from a charge of No. 8's. An ounce of No. 8 shot contains more than 400 pellets and an ounce of No. 6 shot less than 225. You make the choice.

And so to gun specifics. I can't knock the 12-gauge. My Remington Model 870, 12-gauge pump has accounted for more partridge than any two of my other guns, for the simple reason that it was the only good gun I had for a long time. But I have to admit that the grouse shooter just doesn't need all a 12-gauge has to offer.

Admittedly, you will bag a few extra birds with a 12-gauge, literally as a fringe benefit. (When your hold is sloppy the fringe of a 12-gauge pattern may be enough to knock your birds down.) But ruffed grouse, unlike pheasant and duck, don't take a lot of killing. Could be you'd rather miss clean with a smaller gauge. That's up to you.

I think a 20-gauge is best for this work. Its effective range is just shy of the 12-gauge's and the much lighter weight of the gun and shells is a factor in an all-day hike, at least when a man reaches the age when he starts considering those things. Even the 28-gauge and the .410, in the hands of a crack shot, will fold birds up to twenty-five or thirty yards. Since I'd bet that about 80 per cent of the ruffed grouse I shoot each year *fall* within thirty yards of the gun, it would seem that the tiny bores are adequate for most shooting. You will find a ten-yard shot more common than a fifty-yarder in any but the most unusual cover.

As for gun styling, if a man has the dough to spend on a good double-barrel, that's the traditional piece of ordnance for a grouse gunner to acquire. Some hunters feel that the over-and-under has an edge, since shooters familiar with pumps and autoloaders often prefer a single sighting plane. But for the snap shooting required in the grouse woods, I can't see anything seriously wrong with the side-by-side.

As for myself, like most inveterate shooters I've done lots of switching around. I now favor a 20-gauge Remington 870 on the theory that with interchangeable barrels and a variety of loads I can use it on most everything. Nor will there be any fumbling when I switch to the 12-gauge of the same model for pass shooting at waterfowl, fox hunting and deer hunting with rifled slugs.

I don't mean to slight any other guns. There are plenty of other satisfactory shot-spewers, both domestic and foreign, doing a good job in the uplands. But like other hunters I have to buy my guns. I can't afford them all, and can't use what I don't own.

GROUSE SHOOTING

Of all the upland birds discussed in this book the ruffed grouse is the hardest to hit with any degree of consistency no matter how well you shoot. That's why so many sportsmen rate it the number one sporting bird. They may actually enjoy hunting other species more because they can restore their shooting egos following a bout in the brush with some partridge.

Now, if you are carefully selective about your shots, you can shoot a pretty fair average on Ol' Ruff. But if you bang away, catch-as-catch-can, you will find him the most challenging target in the uplands. Shooting at virtually every grouse that gives you the merest glimpse of him will result in your making some "impossible" hits. It can also add up to a string of miserable misses. But that's the only way you are going to bag many birds.

You are going to miss and you will miss often, largely because you must shoot and shoot often if you are to heft a few of these prizes, put them in your game pocket and eventually prepare them for the table. And the grouse is an excellent table bird. He who does not shoot but stands around open-mouthed, waiting for an "open" shot while this dauntless bird bangs through some seemingly impossible cover, might as well be in the field with an empty gun.

There are two major things that will cause a man to miss in the grouse woods: (1) trying to lead the bird; (2) lifting cheek from the comb of the gunstock.

Forget everything you've read and been told about leading. Partridge hunting is a "poke and hope" proposition. Spot him over the bead at the end of your barrel—or even black him out with the barrel—and jerk that trigger. The natural momentum of your swing will furnish you all the "lead" you need.

If you consciously try to lead the bird, you will find that you have led yourself right into shooting into a tree or a clump of brush; or, worse, you will establish your lead and then stop your swing. A stationary gun barrel will never throw a shot charge that will intercept a flying bird—unless the bird accidentally flys into the pattern.

Because it is standard operational procedure for a ruffed grouse to get out of thick cover and to put some shot-absorbing obstacle between him and you an instant after he's broken clear, this up-land bomber more than any other bird tempts a man to "peek" over his gun barrel in an attempt to locate him. Don't!

The gun barrel, not your eyes, should locate that bird. It can do it properly and with dispatch only if you have the comb buried into your cheek. Keeping that stock tight against your face will automatically align eye and gun barrel.

To do this properly takes much practice. No grouse hunter should have to think about properly mounting his gun. It must be a reflex action, as unthinking and almost as quick as a squint when bright sunlight breaks through the cover.

Almost invariably a ruffed grouse is a rising target. Don't worry about shooting over the top of him. You will be shooting under. That's why many successful partridge shooters actually do not see the bird they connect with when they fire since they have covered him with the gun barrel. If you can see some sky between the bird and the bead when you touch off you've just missed a bird.

The exception to this rule is when budding grouse flush from trees. Then the bird's course is a slant downward. You must shoot under. You can get some practice at this by shooting the high house in skeet from stations 1 and 2. If you want to learn gun mounting and increase your partridge score, when shooting skeet mount your gun *after* you call for your bird.

Ruffed grouse often like to "bud" (sit in poplar trees and eat their buds) when snow and cold lock up the land. So should you hunt at that time of year, expect to hear them burst out of trees, or spot them sitting on a limb as well as erupting out of a snow bank where they've roosted for the night.

I'd bet that even more partridge are missed when they flit out of a tree than are missed when they get up out of cover, and that number is considerable. It's a disconcerting occurrence but a sporting shot. Shooting them while they are sitting in trees is something else again, although I must confess to doing it upon occasion, when a long string of misses has converted me into a partridge-hater seeking revenge and some proof to convince my wife that I've really been hunting.

If you miss a grouse the first time and he's still in sight don't hesitate to touch off again. Sometimes that excited second shot will get him because you are doing what comes naturally, hurriedly swinging through the bird and touching off. Hunters miss birds when they start thinking about what they ought to do.

Infrequently, but a number of times a year, I kill grouse with a third shot. This happens almost invariably when I touch off my first shot before I've even gotten the gun mounted. Sure, I'm anxious and shooting too fast. But I've also killed grouse shooting from the hip. My mortal fear always is that the one quick shot is the only one I'm going to get at him. Just remember that the second and third shots may come as an unexpected bonus. But if you don't get into the expensive habit of touching off quick you won't do much shooting. If you aren't going to shoot there's no sense carrying that gun all day.

Fortunately, most shots at partridge are one at a time things. If they got up like quail, in coveys, there'd be even fewer killed than there are now. Early in the season, before the family groups have broken up, you may bump into coveys of ruffed grouse. But seldom do they all erupt at once, as quail do. They like to flit out one or two at a time.

This can be disconcerting too. A grouse flush under this situation often finds a man who has just shot at the first or second bird that got out now in the process of reloading or making some remark to his companion. He may go all to pieces trying to get on the third one that goes out and so on.

There is one thing a man has going for him in that situation. Usually the coveys are made up mostly of birds hatched that spring. These young birds are not the strong, fast flyers the adults are and therefore present an easier target. By far the bulk of the "doubles," and that "hat trick" of partridge hunting, the occasional "triple," are scored on these fluttery "squeakers."

Finally, even though a bird disappears behind a screen of cover, if you're ready to touch off that shot, let it loose. If you've swung with the bird and his flight pattern hasn't deviated you may be lucky enough to ram a few pellets through the screen and get him. For all their bombast and craftiness, ruffed grouse aren't hard to knock down. A couple of pellets will put them on the ground.

So if there is any secret to successful ruffed-grouse shooting it is to shoot and shoot again. Be proud of any bird you knock down and display a big limit to anyone who'll look.

There's only one thing you shouldn't do. Don't keep track of the number of shells expended in comparison to the number of birds bagged. If you do you'll wind up a pool player.

2
Ol' Fancy Pants
THE PHEASANT

BRASH, gaudy and noisy, the cock pheasant is an easy mark for slurs from sophisticated hunters for he makes a large and sometimes lumbering target for dedicated wingshooters.

But while the big Oriental bird has his detractors, he also has a lot going for him—enough to make him one of the most sought-after game birds on the North American continent.

Considering his size, his relative slowness while getting airborne and his willingness to beat his way across open expanses of air rather than dodging behind the first available cover, the pheasant should be one of the easiest targets in the uplands. But somehow, hunters manage to miss more than their share of cackling roosters.

One of the reasons pheasants are so often missed is the desire that grips thousands of otherwise casual hunters to knock down at least one bird like this every season. Probably more hunters who know less about hunting and spend less time gun-swinging pursue pheasant than go after any of our other upland species.

Pheasants are popular with the weekend or once-a-season hunter because they are large and colorful and the successful hunter likes to display his bag. Other game birds are also beautiful upon close examination but appear drab at first glance. The pheasant stands out—even at a distance.

In addition, the pheasant is a fine "table bird." There's a lot of meat there, virtually chicken sized, and a bird is worth cleaning.

With its large breast and big drumsticks, not only is there quantity to pheasant but the quality is high.

Finally the pheasant is available. In his wild state he is a bird of the crop lands, not the wilderness. In such climes as South Dakota and Nebraska, where he has flourished, the pheasant has progressed from near-nuisance status to an important economic asset that attracts swarms of hunters from all over the continent. In other states he may be accorded almost trophy-bird status, with bag limits that allow only one or two cock birds per day. Because of the color differentiation it is possible to set up laws protecting hens.

Part of the pheasant's availability stems from the fact that this bird is the easiest to introduce artificially into "shot-out" areas, or places that normally don't hold birds. This leads conservation departments to utilize the bird to furnish supplemental hunting for its hunting license buyers and permits private landowners to stock their holdings with pheasants for fee shooting. Pheasants have the facility of becoming virtually as wild as their naturally reared counterparts within hours of their release from holding crates, a trait unusual in pen-raised birds.

From all this you may erroneously conclude that I am damning pheasants with faint praise. I'm not. For I have a profound admiration for a bird that will get up from underfoot, will boldly and vocally tell you just what he thinks of you and then defy you, sometimes successfully, to make that easy shot.

The way pheasants often skulk and refuse to get off the ground, preferring to run rather than fly, and their frequent unwillingness to sit tight for pointing dogs are irritants. But these are minor matters, either to be solved by using the proper dog or dogs, or to be put up with and chuckled over. No matter how long and how much they've shot them, few are the hunters who can turn down an invitation for a pheasant shoot.

The pheasant we shoot in the United States today is a combination of strains imported from the Orient and first successfully introduced in Oregon in 1881. The major strains which make up the *Phasianus colchicus torquatus* (Ol' John Pheasant) are the Mongolian, Chinese and English ringneck, and Mutant.

There has never been a successful introduction of pheasant in the wild in the Deep South. But despite the pheasant's inability to adapt to conditions in that part of the country, so popular is this bird that many shooting areas in the South offer gunning on stocked birds for the pleasure of hunters.

The king-sized rooster pheasant may hit almost five pounds, live weight, but the average is probably a bit under three pounds. With relatively small wings for this body weight the bird is slow in getting underway, but once it hits its peak and levels off in a straight line it can move at speeds up to forty miles per hour. Pheasants have a tendency to glide when they've reached maximum momentum. They are often missed by shooters while in this long glide because they are imperceptibly pitching down.

There is no mistaking the cock pheasant for any other game bird in the wild. His bright coloration, streaming tail feathers and raucous "Cawk! Cawk! Cawk!" as he gets airborne set him off from all others.

The hen is a bird of a different color. Brownish and mottled, she is drab in comparison to the multi-colored cock and much smaller as a rule. Early in the hunting seasons, before the immature cocks have "colored out," it can be hard to tell a rooster from a hen. Even the cackle is no absolutely positive identification, although most hunters will depend upon it. On occasion hens, as well as cocks, will cackle when they get into the air. Since hens are usually protected, make sure you can positively identify a cock before shooting to save yourself some money and embarrassment.

Both birds have long tails, but while the cock's streams grace-fully out behind in flight, the hen's tail often presents a somewhat awkward appearance. The hen bird can be confused with ruffed grouse and sharp-tailed grouse when flushed in thick cover, and in some areas the range of these birds overlaps.

If there is one game bird in the world that refuses to "lose his cool," it's the cock pheasant. He'll strut in front of you, defy you and escape you with the dash of an old time buccaneer. His manner has earned this swashbuckler of the uplands the reputation of a rogue.

There is only one way to beat a rogue on his own ground. That's to be bolder, smarter and more persistent than he.

A shy lad, they say, makes no time with blondes. Likewise, the cautious hunter will kill few pheasants.

In plain English, if you want to be a successful pheasant hunter you must either overwhelm or outsmart the crafty critter. The first procedure will probably result in the biggest bag of birds, the second the most fun and the greatest test of your hunting ability.

In good pheasant country (and there are at least little pockets of good pheasant venue in practically all the Northern states) there'll be no great problem of finding out "where are the birds" as in ruffed-grouse hunting.

Everyone from the first-grade pupils in the country school to the mayor of the hamlet at the crossroads will know where the pheasants are. These jokers are not shy, retiring creatures. They strut their stuff for all to see—when a man's dog is home in the kennel and his shotgun freshly oiled and racked.

The two problems that face a pheasant hunter are: (1) finding a place to hunt; (2) getting the big birds into the air. Most pheasant hunting is done on or adjacent to farm lands. In fact, when things get tough during the winter, pheasants have been known to come into the barnyard and compete with the domestic chickens for scratch and pickings from the manure. It has been claimed that pheasants, traditionally bold, have hybridized with chickens, turkeys and other domestic fowl.

This way of life by a wild game bird can cause a hunter grief in two ways. First of all, landowners, particularly those who are growing a crop, have become increasingly reluctant to allow hunters and their dogs to traipse across their holdings. And if there's no crop there won't be many birds, for they like grain. Secondly, many farmers develop not only a proprietary interest in the birds they see every day but they actually become fond of them. They don't like to see them shot.

So, unless you do your pheasant hunting on well-planned trips far from home where guides, lodging, place to hunt and so on are worked out ahead of time, your first step in successful pheasant hunting is to get next to a landowner.

How each hunter obtains permission to hunt private lands must remain his own secret. I have no advice to give because I have no desire to run into you some day in a cornfield I thought was exclusively my own. But heed this. If you treat a landowner as you would a friend or a business associate, and forget about him being a "dumb farmer," you may find the door opens without sticking.

Once you're on the land you face the problems of getting the birds out of the cover so you can shoot them. Those attention-attracting rooster pheasants that everyone saw along the roadsides scratching gravel, flying into roost at night or pecking in the stubble have suddenly vanished. No bird can be so bold one minute and so circumspect the next.

There is only one sure way to produce pheasants and that's by using a dog. I'm hepped on the subject of using dogs on game birds because I know it works. (We'll be going into dogs, what kind to use on what birds and so on, in Chapter 10.) But bear in mind that unless you have a hunting dog of some kind with you, there's little chance you'll recover a pheasant once you knock it down.

So, with the aid of your dog, you must overwhelm or outsmart the pheasant. Take the overwhelming method first. I'd question whether one should call it a hunt or simply a shoot when this is done; but in certain situations, it is the only way that pheasants will be produced, and if you enjoy hunting in large parties, it's about the only way a pheasant hunt can be managed.

Pheasants are notorious for their unwillingness to resort to their wings until all other methods of eluding a hunter and dog have failed. In comparison with most of the other upland birds they have relatively stubby wings for their length of almost a yard, but their legs are made for sprinting and they use them.

Thus parties must hunt pheasants almost as they would deer, in groups divided up between "drivers" and "standers." This takes some organization and one of the hunters must boss this hunting gang or everyone will be wandering off. Unless the hunters work in unison, birds will sneak back during the drive and the shooting will be poor.

Here's how it works.

When a cornfield, highly grassed soil-bank land, a big cattail marsh (late in the season) or other suitable cover is located and permission obtained to hunt it, the party of hunters breaks up into two groups. About one-third of the group will go to one end of the cornfield, preferably downwind. When these hunters have stationed themselves, the larger section of the party spreads out ten to twenty corn rows apart, depending upon how well the corn has been cultivated, and starts moving toward the standers.

This type of hunt is commonly carried on successfully without a dog. When a dog is used he should be a very well-trained retriever or spaniel that will walk at heel until ordered out to retrieve, or that is under enough control to work back and forth within gun range. Because of the number of persons in the hunting party and their positioning, some shots will be provided by even an uncontrollable dog, but more will be spoiled.

The idea is to push the birds down toward the standers at the end of the field. Pheasants will skulk ahead of the hunters, scooting down the corn rows until they run out of cover. Then, caught between drivers and standers, they will take to the air. So the heavy shooting comes when the drivers near the end of the field, about the last fifty yards.

Of course, there can be sporadic shooting in between, for the birds will try to double back between the drivers. Many will succeed, living to outwit a hunter another day. Others will get anxious, however, if the drivers go slow and easy, stopping often to break their walking pace. When these birds get up they can provide tricky shooting.

Dogs can be dispensed with on this type of hunt, but when properly trained they can be a great aid in keeping the birds moving ahead of the drivers or rousting into the air roosters that try to cut back. Also, if the cornfield is weed-choked, birds will sit tight in concealment and let a hunter walk past. A good dog will put them into flight. Furthermore, the heavier the undergrowth, the more vital a dog will be in the recovery of downed birds.

To some extent this is one of the few dangerous ways to upland bird-hunt. A group of gunners is concentrated in a given area, then split into two groups and aimed at each other. The cover may be difficult to see over or through, and the game bird has a tendency to stay on the ground or fly flat. It's a situation that can lead to members of the party spraying each other with shot unless every precaution is taken.

Hunters in the party must be made to understand that running birds are not to be ground-swatted, and even when a bird is in flight, firing should not commence until it has at least cleared the cornstalk tops. Every man should know the location of the drivers next to him and the standers out front.

. So much for overwhelming the pheasant. There are a few other variations of this, including driving rural roads in an automobile, spotting birds along the roadside and getting out of the car to hunt them. (Pheasants are not near as likely to stand around and get potted on the ground as ruffed grouse. They are sophisticated birds and usually duck for cover when a car stops.)

In some parts of the country where the terrain allows it, hunters have been known to chase pheasants in jeeps and pick-up trucks. Generally a pheasant will fly from about an eighth to a quarter-mile maximum. After several such successive flights birds will stay on the ground out of sheer exhaustion and can be easily shot or picked up by hand.

Those are versions of mechanically overpowering the birds. Now let's touch on trying to outsmart them, although I'm not sure I ever outsmarted a pheasant in my life. Usually it was persistence, luck or perhaps the fact that the bird just got tired of playing games with me only to have his derisive cackle and rattle of wings against the marsh grass turned into an epitaph by an ounce and a quarter of No. 5 shot.

For the sportsman who hunts alone, with one or two companions or, best of all, in the company of his dog, I have an important word of advice. *Don't be afraid to get your feet wet.* This is meant both literally and figuratively.

Pheasants will hide in some pretty strange and impossible places. So don't hesitate about going on a fool's errand in the hope of getting a bird, when the "sure bets" have failed to pay off. For after a few days of hunting pressure have been applied to John Pheasant, you may literally have to get your feet wet if you are to shoot your share of birds.

Marshes are a great place to hunt pheasants, if there are any in the vicinity. This can mean little half-acre potholes or large expanses of waving marsh vegetation. You will find birds around the edges of the pothole areas or way out in the large marshes, where they'll perch up on hummocks or on the small islands of

40

solid footing that usually dot these large areas. Late in the season, after ice makes walking easy, you will find pheasants in the cattail marshes. They are favorite winter cover.

When you find grain fields adjacent to rough cover such as marshes, creek bottoms, overgrown soil banks, shallow ditches, unmowed strips of hay or canary grass, or small islands of brush, you've found yourself a season-long pheasant heaven.

When a man's time is limited or he doesn't have a capable dog to work the marshes and thick stuff he should hunt early in the morning, state laws permitting. For the birds hang in the heavy cover during the middle of the day and unless a dog roots them out, it's only a matter of luck if a couple of hunters get one into the air.

Pheasants start moving from their nighttime roosting places just as the sun is starting up over the horizon. They come out to dry off and to pick gravel for their crops. This concentrates them along rural roads or in open fields that can be viewed from roads. They are so vulnerable at this time of day that some states set the legal hour for shooting late in the morning, and on opening day starting time is usually set after midday.

From there birds start to spread out to feed, cornfields being a favorite feeding area during most of the hunting season. If there's any cover at all, picked or rolled cornfields may be more profitable to work than the standing, unpicked fields. Birds may hang in among the dry, noisy stalks all day, feeding on the corn on the ground, flattening themselves to become invisible on nearly bare ground or skulking in carelessly cultivated rows.

But there will be other places the pheasant feeds. He'll eat almost any kind of weed seed, so overgrown fields are a good bet. He'll also make out on grain of any kind—I've opened crops that contained acorns and nuts of various kinds, aquatic tubers and even willow twigs. He'll even glean dried grasshopper and cricket husks, but this is desperation food.

The hunter and his dog or a pair of hunting buddies had best hunt the small-cover stands and leave the large fields to the gangs of hunters. For pheasants will kite down a corn row and flush wild if there are no standers. Even when marked down this means a long hike before a chance is afforded to put him up again.

The pheasant hunter who bog-trots during the middle of the

day is one of the hardest working sportsmen in the field and deserves every bird he shoots. The going is swampy. This means added effort to lift one's legs up and through the sloppy tangles. Even on the edges and on the islands where the walking is relatively good, the cover will be thick and the shooting as tricky as any a pheasant can provide.

While it is preferable to work every bit of cover available, where the going is soft and wet there should be some preferred objectives. These are the willow, tag alder, red osier and other brush thickets that dot marshes or line creek banks. They not only provide shade and protection during the loafing (for birds) part of the day, but are usually dry enough to lay up on. Pheasants gravitate to these clumps, for despite their proclivity for wet, low places they are not aquatic.

Pheasants don't really care to get their feet wet. But they're smart enough to pick resting spots that make a man get his wet if he's going to get to them.

PHEASANT GUNS AND LOADS

Every now and then, when convivial strangers who share an interest in hunting get together, some egotist who wants to make an impression will announce solemnly: "I kill all my pheasants with a .410 and No. 8 shot," or words to that effect.

This makes an impression all right. But unless this guy is the reincarnation of Ad Topperwein, Herb Parsons, Bill Johnson or some other top-flight exhibition shooter from one of the major arms companies my reaction is one of incredulous disgust.

Not that a man can't kill a pheasant or two with a small-bore shotgun like the .410 or 28-gauge, if he selects his birds and is an accomplished shot. But if he's a normal hunter, he's not choosy and is a poor to piddlin' shot. If he uses this kind of equipment he will send "missed" birds off to die or fall easy prey to predators.

The pheasant is one of the few upland birds that should be hunted with a 12-gauge in preference to all others, and the only primers that should be popped are those that ignite a maximum change of relatively coarse shot.

These colorful pirates of the meadows and marshes are big and they're tough. They can lug away a lot of shot. Even when they bounce hard off the ground, if there's an ounce of life left in them they are off and running or struggling to reach concealment.

That means a big gun and a heavy load. And unless the shooting is done over a well-broke, experienced and proven-on-pheasants pointing dog, it also means at least a modified choke or, even better, a full choke. This will be discussed more fully in the chapter on dogs. But only a minority of pheasants are shot over points. Even when this is done a shooter can take his time getting on a slow rising bird, or ride it out to take advantage of the tight pattern a full choke affords at forty yards.

In general, however, pheasants will provide the "longest shooting" of any of our upland game birds. The object of sport shooting is to kill cleanly. Tough cock pheasants are hard to nail solidly or break up enough so they can't get away. So the gun and load you use for waterfowl hunting will be a more sensible bet than your favorite on quail, ruffed grouse or woodcock.

Let's go into some reasons. The pheasant, a big bird that is not at all reluctant to fly out into the open, offering a clear silhouettte, is going to require energy and shot concentration. That's what you get with a full-choked 12-gauge spewing out one and a quarter ounces of No. 4, 5 or 6 shot propelled by three and three quarters drams equivalent of powder. A gun of substantial heft, a barrel of 28 or even 30 inches and a single sighting plane helps a shooter swing and keep swinging on a bird. That's the reason you'll see more pump and autoloading shell shuckers in the cornfields of the Midwest than any other type of gun.

The hunter who works any kind of a dog and isn't part of a gang hunt can legitimately use a 20-gauge. He gets a nod of approval if it's chambered for 3-inch shells and he uses them. This puts the smaller bore in the same class as the 12-gauge. But if he does much shooting, the lighter 20 with the heavy loads is going to give him a headache or a sore shoulder. The 16-gauge is a compromise gun, no better, no worse than the 12 or 20, depending upon the shot charge in the fodder that's fed it.

I'll concede a number of exceptions to the "big gun, heavy load" axiom for pheasant shooters, but never to the shooters in the organized pheasant drives. This is probably the most popular way of hunting the birds so it is a general recommendation for the man out to buy a pheasant gun. If a double-barrel gun is used, the set of barrels for pheasant hunting should be bored modified and full.

Oh! I suppose there's even an exception here—if it becomes a matter of necessity in order to defend your good name.

Art Reid, a fellow outdoor writer from Carbondale, Ill., and I got involved in a pheasant shoot over an expanse of Illinois prairie land. The cornstalks had been knocked down and I'd have bet dollars to doughnuts there wasn't a bird in the whole damn section. It was clean farmed country; with no standing corn it looked as desolate and devoid of game as a ping-pong parlor.

But that rolled cornfield was the only thing the pheasants had to go on—and they did right well. The others in our party were strangers to us. We got a couple birds on dogless drives but we were actually walking past some birds in the sparse cover.

They finally let me unlimber my fiery, young Springer spaniel. This really didn't help. She found the tight sitters, but she'd get carried away with the shooting and the birds running unimpeded in the open rows. We really needed long-shooting guns! So I put her up and put down a more docile, better-trained Labrador.

That's when we started getting birds. Alternately walking at heel, to do the picking up when a bird spooked and was shot, and then being sent out to cast back and forth across the line of hunters (and sometimes behind us) he put the skulkers into the air.

One of the hunters in the group turned out to be a "bird claimer." Everything that got up he shot at and claimed he hit. (Let's be charitable. Maybe he did. But *if* he did, this gentleman was to pheasants what Sgt. Alvin York was to the Kaiser's infantrymen.) Because my own dog naturally gravitated more or less to me, occasionally there were some pheasants getting out close to me. That's the one time I wished I had had a more open barrel on the shotgun—to pop those big birds on the rise before our bird claiming friend could unlimber his weapon.

But maybe we cured him of sucking eggs. I hope so. At least he knew by the hunt's end that not everyone believed him. For while there aren't a whole lot of manners displayed in any type of gang hunt, and there's always a lot of good-natured raillery exchanged about who shot what, to shoot at birds far out of range and seriously assert you've hit them is a breach of manners.

Quick handling, short-barreled, light guns that throw a well-dispersed pattern of fine shot have a purpose in the uplands. They are for small, quick birds that require virtually instinctive shooting from up close. The center of this type of pattern may down a pheasant but won't really nail him, and the fringes will only "tickle" him, resulting in a sick but unrecovered bird.

Bear in mind that although the hunter who has allowed the hardware store salesman to sell him a full-choke gun and magnum loads is over-gunned and over-loaded for most upland game, he is on a better track when it comes to pheasant gunning than the man who thinks it's the mark of a sportsman to peck away at these rugged, hard-to-stop rascals with a pop gun.

PHEASANT SHOOTING

When gunning pheasants there is only one thing to remember. You've all the time in the world. Use it to your advantage. *Do not hurry your shot.*

Oh, if I could only take the advice I dish out! To follow it I have to work at it. But believe me, the deadliest pheasant shot is the calm, collected character who comes up smoothly, swings through steadily and deliberately, and folds up his birds with a well-placed charge out in front of them.

Pheasants must be led. Because they are big birds and have long tails they are deceptive. Too many hunters load a bird's tail with shot only to have him shudder but keep right on going. Birds only fringed by a pattern may never give any indication that they are hit.

Furthermore, because pheasants usually pound their way across open country making their escape, or glide down from the open as they drop into cover, they can be killed at incredibly long distances by the man who will establish the proper lead and keep his barrel swinging.

45

I used to do a little hunting with a professional football player, Urban Henry, when he was with the Green Bay Packers. A giant of a man, he was armed with a Browning autoloader with a full-choked, 32-inch barrel. He dropped a cock pheasant one time that fell 92 paces from where he fired. Sure, it was a phenomenal or lucky shot—but I saw the man drop other birds at distances where it didn't seem worthwhile to even raise the gun.

My own longest shot was scored on a pheasant clawing for altitude and topping a screen of trees. It was with a 20-gauge Remington pump, full-choke 28-inch barrel and a magnum load of one-and-one-eighth ounces of No. 4 shot.

I missed the first two shots I touched off, swore to myself, and then pushed out about three axe-handles above the climbing bird and jerked. He folded. My Labrador had to catch him, but he was well hit. The treetop was about forty feet high and we paced off seventy paces from where I shot to the base. (Name of witness furnished on request.)

I cite these examples to illustrate the importance of lead. Pheasant shooting is open shooting. Sure, if you hunt alone, or with a companion and a dog, you will put birds out of dense cover, tag alder, cedar swamps, etc. Then you must adjust and shoot as you would on ruffed grouse—poke and hope.

But for the most part, the bird will present a crisp, clean target against the sky. You can pick the time and the place you want to rap him. How can you miss? It's easy. Not enough lead. Nobody *overleads* a pheasant.

Then too, the pheasant can be a tricky target, both because he's the bird he is and because of the way he is hunted. On a pheasant drive, both drivers and standers may find themselves presented with shots that are going away, incoming, at right angles or quartering to the side. This calls for some masterful gun swinging. There is no predicting just which way he'll get up or whether he will tower or decide to go flat out when he's confronted with a dog and a couple of hunters. So pheasants can be missed.

Perhaps it's appropriate here to remind you that wing shooting is customarily done by one of two methods. These two styles of shooting are called by many different names but for our purposes let's call them "pointing out" and "swinging through."

The shooter who points out makes a quick calculation of the lead he thinks will be required to intercept the bird, gets his gun out there ahead of the bird, and keeps it swinging at that distance in front of the bird until he pulls the trigger. If he's estimated the lead correctly the bird folds.

This style of shooting will work on pheasant and, to a lesser extent, on sharp-tailed grouse, prairie chicken, maybe Hungarian partridge. It's a fine way to shoot waterfowl. But it's near worthless on ruffed grouse, woodcock and quail. That's why I prefer the swing-through style for shooting the uplands. It's more versatile, and adaptable to every game species.

In swing-through shooting, the gunner mounts the gun as he follows the flight of the bird with his eyes; as he aligns eye and gun barrel he comes up from behind the bird and swings through it, and as the barrel passes ahead of the bird he touches off. The speed at which he swings the barrel correlates automatically with the speed of the flying bird. If he keeps that barrel swinging, the time lapse between the brain saying "pull" and the trigger finger doing it provides him with a built-in lead.

I find this method deadly out to forty yards. Beyond that, a man has no business shooting anyway. But if you do try some real long shots, you will learn to pull after you have swung some distance past the head of the bird instead of just as you go through; or actually to lose sight of the bird under your barrel, shooting at a straightaway rising bird.

Whatever system you use (and if it's successful, don't change) the secret is *keeping that gun barrel moving*. If you let it stop, the bird will fly away from the pattern. I think most shooters tend to stop a gun more often when they use the pointing-out method, since once they have established what they think is the right lead, their inclination is to stop and expect the bird to fly into the pattern.

When shooting is done in gangs it is more sporting (and provides shooting for more people in case the nearest shooter misses) if the bird is allowed to reach altitude and get out a ways. It is also a safety measure. If you should get a safe opportunity at a bird that has gone into a glide, just remember that even if you can't detect it, the gliding bird is dropping. If his wings are still beating he will be rising at least slightly.

The lone hunter who works with his dog won't have to worry about drivers and standers whom he might sprinkle with shot. If he's quick and is hunting with a flushing dog, which may put the bird out some distance in front of him, it is still a sporting shot to take the bird on its initial rise. Once a flushed bird has leveled off and is in full flight, it takes some real gun-swinging to catch up with him and bring him down.

Over a pointing dog, if shooting a full-choke gun, the sporting thing is to let the bird get out a little way, in full flight. Shooting at a bird ten to twenty yards out front, if the full-choke pattern connects, will riddle him. With an open-bored gun, probably the best time to take the bird is just as he tops his rise and straightens out. He'll be close enough for the more open pattern to be effective and for just an instant will hang up in the air. This shot is the world's easiest, requires little or no lead and light loads will do the job.

But generally, get out in front of those birds and hit them solidly with a dense pattern of No. 6 or larger shot. Pheasants can soak up a lot of shot and cripples don't give up easily; unless you kill cleanly, you are going to waste a lot of wonderful birds that could have given others pleasure in flight or in the roaster.

3
A Gentleman's Gentleman
THE BOBWHITE QUAIL

The Bobwhite Quail

THE very antithesis of the ringneck pheasant is the bobwhite quail.

Before that fancy phrase scares you off, let me explain. I can't think of any other way to sum up the difference in a sentence. For the honest and gentlemanly bobwhite (*Colinus virginianus*) is to the roistering and double-dealing pheasant what George Washington is to Jean Lafitte.

Just as readers of history can admire both the honorable "father of his country" and the devious pirate, each for his own personality, so hunters have enjoyed Bob White and John Pheasant because they are so unlike. And while pheasants are pursued by more hunters each season than any other upland game birds, there's little doubt that more quail are killed by shotgunners than any comparable target, making them the two most popular upland species.

The stronghold of the bobwhite is the South, where hunting seasons are long and bag limits liberal. Even in the North (and there is also some good quail hunting to be had in the East and Midwest) because the Bob is a small bird, daily limits are more generous than with the large pheasant. The basis for this may be predicated on an estimating of what it takes to make a meal, and the fact that shooting opportunities on quail usually come in multiples rather than singly. Few hunters could be asked to settle for one bird on a covey rise.

51

In many parts of the South, quail are called "pottage" (partridge), but for the most part they are known plainly and simply as "buhds" (birds). Mention "bird hunting" anywhere from the Carolinas to Texas and only a fool will ask, "what kind?" In their native range, to the hunter, there is only one kind of bird—the bobwhite quail.

Always a gentleman, the bobwhite is predictable, and no bird lies better to a pointing dog. These factors, along with large numbers and wide distribution, make quail a readily available and easy bird to hunt.

The bird is not quite the same the country over, and it is a great oversimplification to say that there are only two ways to hunt quail, either afoot or on horseback. The conditions and hunting techniques that apply in Alabama's "black belt" are hardly identical to the mode of hunting in the Florida palmettos, the Missouri and Arkansas Ozarks, Illinois' southern extremity, Pennsylvania's hills or an Iowa cornfield.

At the risk of being accused of being a man of inherited means (rather than a self-made pile of shotgun hulls), I'd like to say that the "real way to go," when it comes to quail hunting, is playing the gentleman's game: hunting the gentleman's bird by following a wide-ranging brace of Pointers on horseback over a large plantation.

At the same time, not a day would I trade for that kind of hunting which has been, and will be, spent riddling blackjack oaks with fine shot while trying to hit a critter than can also be found in the southern equivalent of northern ruffed grouse cover, putting miles on boot soles and shredding pants fronts. It's all a matter of terrain and choice.

In some ways it can be claimed that quail resemble pheasants. To an extent, hunters may find the same problems when they seek either bird. Because the quail also prefers agricultural lands, finding a place to hunt may pose a problem, although usually this is not as severe as the case might be with pheasants. The experienced hunter can often pick a cock from a hen bird even in flight.

While a knowledgeable hunter may be able to scout some strange ruffed grouse and pheasant country and stand a fair chance of locating some game, the bobwhite hunter will do an awful lot of wheel spinning if he doesn't hunt familiar grounds or get local help.

Staying "close to home" is a bobwhite characteristic, and certain coveys can be depended upon to show up within an easily defined area. Knowing about the "sawdust pile" covey, the "crick bottom" covey and so on saves a lot of time and makes hunting easier and more productive.

To any halfway experienced observer, the only bird that might possibly be confused with a quail in flight is the meadow lark, which shows white tail feathers in flight. However, I have heard fairly experienced hunters, encountering a bird strange to them, call Hungarian partridge "quail."

Furthermore, ornithologists and even some country boy hunters can tell you there are several varieties of bobwhite, including the most common Eastern bobwhite, the Florida bobwhite and the Texas bobwhite, and there has been considerable hybridization.

At an average of less than half a pound (five to six ounces) the bobwhite ranks as one of our smaller upland game species. The white throat and head markings of the cock bird distinguish it from the yellowish (buffy) marking of these parts on a hen, although at times a clear color line, and henceforth the sex, is hard to determine.

The whistling call of the bobwhite is to the rural areas of the South what the reverberating drum of a ruffed grouse on a log is to the northern timberlands. Gregarious, the birds will usually be found in coveys (any group of birds of three or more), and they will run if need be. But aided by the confusion caused in a whirring covey flush, they can make their escape by rising, at getaway speeds up to forty miles per hour, then alternately beating and gliding to slant down into the nearest available cover.

The gentleman bobwhite is such a good sport about his role in the relationship between hunter, dog and game that he ranks as the most enjoyable bird to hunt that either the casual or dedicated nimrod will encounter.

QUAIL-HUNTING TACTICS

Quail hunting brings out the best in man. It is a sport for gentle-men, natural-born or self-made. Perhaps this aura stems from its Southern traditions; but if it has, the attitude toward the hunt and a day in the field has spread to the border and northern states that also offer the bobwhite as a legal target.

While doing a considerable amount of quail hunting in a number of our states, never have I gone out with a quail hunter who was not a gentleman. What these men might have been in private or public life I have no way of knowing. All I know is that they were enjoyable, gentlemanly companions on a bird hunt.

Perhaps it's the fact that dogs are so wedded to quail hunting that keeps this kind of bird hunting on a high plane. Can you ever remember hearing a quail-hunting story that did not involve dogs? It's been my experience that any man who spends time and energy on training dogs will hunt in a sportsmanlike manner and insist that things be done the right way.

Practically every other game bird we know can be hunted with at least limited success by a man or men without dogs. Possibly so can bobwhite quail. But I've never heard of it and what's more important have never done it. So I can't tell you how to do it.

The classic quail hunt is carried out in the Southern tradition, on a large plantation on which the owner "shoots," or leases the hunting rights if he is not a hunter himself. This is the facet of the sport involving fine horses, wide-ranging bird dogs, Negro scouts and helpers, and a strict observance of decorum.

While a proportionately small number of sportsmen are able to hunt regularly in this manner, a quail lease of four thousand acres or less being considered rather small potatoes, I can only say that if you ever get an invitation to hunt this way, snap it up—even though you may have an aversion to straddling a horse. (If you are an impossibly poor rider, arrangements will probably be made for you to ride on a mule or horse-drawn wagon. The wagon will also contain extra dogs and the makings for your noon meal, if the hunt is set up so you'll be out in the field at that time.)

Your cavalcade will probably head cross-country around 9 A.M. after the frost has dissipated, with the dogs reaching out across the sedge grass fields, skimming the brushy draws and coursing through the pine stands. These will be the "biggest-going" practical hunting dogs you'll ever see. If one should run out of the country or disappear, a scout will be dispatched to either round him up or locate him on point.

But your first point comes when you emerge from the pines and start down a gentle slope of the rolling terrain and the white and liver dog slams down, rigid, at the edge of a brushy ditch.

Coming in from the opposite direction the other pointer spots her bracemate and without a word of caution from her handler, stops and honors the find of the first dog. Your party proceeds briskly, but without undue haste, to the dogs.

You're accorded the first crack at the birds and you and another hunter dismount, pull your shotguns from their saddle scabbards, load and walk in on the dogs. You've already walked in ahead of the dog and nothing's happened, so you start looking around on the ground. As you lift your right foot and start to put it down, the world explodes in front of you! It's a big covey, fifteen or sixteen birds. You're caught off-balance, and as you shuffle your feet in an effort to recover, raising your shotgun and your eyes at the same time, you can't make up your mind just what to do.

You do what, at that wild moment, seems the only sensible thing to do—you touch off a round where the birds are thickest. When nothing falls, you stand open-mouthed, forgetting you have another barrel left. By the time you recover, the birds have all scattered, and are either behind cover or pitching down.

Just as you turn apologetically to your host, a straggler bird flushes to your right, your shooting partner's side. You fumble with the safety before touching off a futile shot.

It's little consolation to you when you hear the dog handler crooning to his charges, "Day-ud! Sam. Close, boy. Hunt close. Day-ud!" Your shooting partner, cooler and more experienced, managed to down a pair out of the covey rise, taking them one bird at a time.

After the dead birds are recovered, you remount, the dogs are cast off again and you look for another covey. Seldom are singles diligently hunted on a plantation style hunt. The object is to find the coveys, the bunches of birds.

You lay up over the midday, eating lunch and enjoying the talk about dogs, dog work, good horses, hits and misses. For by this time, having had a chance to work on five more coveys of birds, you've done right on several and lucked out on a couple more of these rocketing little gentlemen. Sometime after 2 P.M. you're off again to hunt for the rest of the "evening," taking advantage of the time when the quail are moving.

Now, if the above was your introduction to quail hunting, you can probably be excused for a number of things, and this will be taken into consideration by your host when he sends out next year's invitation list. But the experienced quail hunter will have noted some things which will make him shudder, and if you went out on that hunt having described yourself as a nimrod of note, your performance made a flat-out liar of you.

Quail hunting is full of unwritten laws, many of them indigenous to a certain locality. But regardless of the mode of hunting, whether in the grand manner roughly described above or by several other methods which will be detailed later, there are several universal rules.

You made your first error, after you had walked in past the dog in the prescribed manner, by looking for the birds on the ground. I can't give you the reason for it. But this throws off a man's shooting, even if he can spot the birds on the ground, which he seldom can. Keep your eyes out front. Then the instant the birds are airborne you'll spot them and can start working on them, regardless of whether they get up right under foot or a bit out in front of you.

Then try, where at all possible, not to be caught off balance. Since any right-handed shooter has to have his left foot advanced and pointing in the direction of the game's flight to shoot effectively, always try to halt in that position. If it's necessary to kick around to flush the birds, do it with your left foot. When you do start stepping with your right foot, get it done in a hurry or be prepared to shift your feet fast so you can attain proper shooting position.

Finally, in your excitement, you took a shot at what was legitimately your shooting partner's bird. Now, if you are with an old hunting buddy and "out for blood" is the game, you can have a ball trying to steal each other's shots and "wipe each other's eye." But generally this just doesn't go.

When a pair of shooters moves in on dogs on point, birds that flare to the right belong to the man at the right and those to the left to the man on the left. If the covey stays bunched, the man on the left works from the middle to the left, and the right-hand shooter works out to the right.

There's more to this than just good manners. It helps prevent "doubling" (both shooters aiming at the same bird), avoiding any question of who shot what; allows a more accurate account of downed birds (a pair of good shooters may put three to six birds on the ground on a covey rise) so they can be recovered by the dog; and keeps gun muzzles swinging away from each hunter, rather than towards them.

But from the standpoint of successful hunting, you made your biggest error right after the birds got out and you decided to shoot into the thick of them. Some people never overcome the fault of "covey" or "flock" shooting. And they never kill many quail.

Even when bunched, there is a lot of air between birds. That's about all you hit, unless your pattern fringe manages to lightly scratch several birds which won't be recovered. To shoot quail out of a rising covey successfully you must concentrate on one bird at a time. Better to kill only one with a single shot than to fire two or three times only to miss or cripple.

There is only one way to learn to do this. That's by hunting quail. Maybe you'll never quite overcome it. Each year the first covey rise usually finds me getting only a lone bird. Why? Because covey rises still shake me up. I start to flock-shoot and then check myself, because I know better; by that time, the first bird I should have shot is long gone. I pull down on a bird, change my mind, start for another only to have it drop to my partner's shot charge, and finally get on a foolish youngster that peeled off to my side and was nothing more than a singles shot.

Therefore, if you value your reputation, it's my suggestion that before you go on the Grand Tour of quail hunting, Southern plantation style, you put in an apprenticeship following a good bird dog on foot.

I'm hesitant about broadly recommending this or that state as a place to go. Hunting cover is never uniform, state-wide, and I assume that only residents of a state know what game is available in what sectors. Non-residents would be foolish to try hunting a state unfamiliar to them without aid from a local hunter or professional guide, just on the basis of a recommendation that Michigan has good ruffed-grouse shooting or South Dakota is tops for pheasant.

With a knowledgeable host, Kansas, Oklahoma and Texas provide quail feasts, plantation-type hunts are best in Alabama, Georgia and Florida and good bets for hunting afoot include Missouri, Arkansas, Iowa, Tennessee and southern Illinois; terrain, cover, birds and practical dogs.

Except that the birds are smaller and therefore seemingly faster and the cover is not quite as thick, hunting in the Ozark foothills or comparable country is not too different from ruffed-grouse hunting. Pointing dogs are by far and away the most popular choice, but flushing dogs can also be utilized.

On a poor day you may have to settle for two or three coveys. On a good day you could hit a dozen to a dozen and a half. But you have really no need for that many coveys to fill out a limit unless your shooting is something you'd rather forget about. For when hunting on foot you also indulge in singles shooting.

After you've shot the covey and have picked up your downed birds you go after the scattered individuals that have separated from the main body as it took off. If you're smart you've marked some of these birds down. But if you were concentrating on your shooting, chances are you'll have only a general idea in what direction the singles went. Then head in that direction and hope your dog can scent and handle a single as well as a covey.

Some dogs who do their best work as far-reaching covey finders don't do too well working singles. Thus very often a dog that will do very well on a plantation-style hunt just won't fill the bill for foot hunting where singles shooting is important.

But let's say that yours is a good singles dog, and he stabs a bird that lit about a hundred yards from where the covey got out. You and your partner march in to kick out the bird.

Here is what should be and is about the easiest shot in upland hunting, except possibly a lone pheasant before a pointing dog. The single bird is right in front of the dog, it will get up almost

from underfoot and take a direction that will be almost straight out from the shooter, no sharp angles. There's no excuse for missing, as with a covey rise. Yet misses occur every day of the quail season.

We'll go into the possible whys in the chapter on how to shoot. But one thing is clear. Until you've mastered this easy shot, you've no business going out on any big-deal hunt or expecting to kill many on a covey rise. And if a shooting companion of yours consistently fails to bring down single birds, you are safe in assuming he'd have a tough job hitting a bull in the butt with a bass fiddle.

You will find quail in some pretty rugged country. And they are great seed eaters. But as was pointed out earlier they are birds of the agricultural lands, not wilderness lovers. While they may leave a roost at dawn, they don't move out far to do much feeding until about mid-morning. By midday they're back in the thickets, dusting or dozing.

Then along about mid-afternoon they move out for their really heavy feeding period before going to the roost at dusk. Should you find birds out and feeding through the middle of the day, it's a pretty good bet there's some bad weather moving in. Quail that feed late in the morning and early in the afternoon may be a problem for the hunter, as well as good weather prognosticators.

Generally, the man who hunts on foot during the middle of the day can enjoy some success by working the thickets, and other resting cover along stream banks, ditches, swamp and timber edges. But when there's some weather coming in they may be passing up their rest time to be out in the fields feeding.

Hill-country farms, regardless of what state they may be in, usually provide good quail habitat, what with corn, soybeans, lespedeza and sesbania right up against small oak stands, overgrown fence rows, brushy gullies and ravines and tangled creek banks. It's rugged walking and tricky shooting, but worth it to the on-foot quail hunter.

You'll find this kind of country and this type of shooting in southern Missouri and northern Arkansas. You may find something very similar in Indiana, Kentucky or Tennessee. Late in the 1950s, in the southwestern hills of my home state, Wisconsin, with a pair of good bird dogs I could find as many as seventeen coveys in an all-day hunt. Decimation by severe winters caused closed seasons for years and restricted hunting when resumed.

There's some excellent quail shooting to be had in the Great Plains states like Nebraska and Kansas. And sportsmen from the tall-corn state of Iowa all the way to Pennsylvania, Maryland and populous New Jersey kill their share of the twenty-five to thirty million bobwhites that are shot each year.

Regardless of *where,* the inveterate on-foot quail shooter knows his day is going to be made up of a lot of hiking. This can be punctuated by rips in his pants from barbed-wire fences, brush slashing his face and scratching his gunstock, and that hopeless feeling when a spooky covey of birds that ran before his dog rather than holding flushes wild before he can come up to within shooting range.

But for every five or ten days when the "luck" was poor to mediocre, the quail hunter will stumble across something like I did when I drove into Bernie Donahue's farm near DeSota, Missouri, a few years back.

Donahue, a professional photographer, had invited Tim Renken, outdoor editor of the *St. Louis Post-Dispatch,* Foin Morrison, a Missouri conservation agent, and me for a hunt on his hundred-and-twenty acre place.

We put down a couple of pretty fair country dogs, Morrison's experienced old pointer male and my graceful and intense little female, and for two and a half hours savored a taste of a quail hunter's heaven.

"I think I've got just an even dozen coveys on the place," Donahue said as we started out. While strolling leisurely along, discussing quail management practices, we enjoyed some of the highest quality dog work I've had on a hunt in a long time and found eleven of those dozen coveys.

On the other hand, you may spend a long afternoon, as I did recently in southern Illinois, in country that from all appearances should have been just as productive as Donahue's farm. My dog made only one covey find and a hunting companion blundered into the birds without seeing the dog. As we started to work out the singles, another companion's dog, described as a "good ol' meat dog," evidenced little interest in birds outside of running them up or refusing to back. That too is part of quail hunting.

There's another kind of specialized quail hunting that I also recommend to you whenever you get the chance. Most commonly done in Florida, a Scout, Jeep, Bronco or some other four-wheel drive swamp buggy supplants the horse as a means of transportation.

Here you'll find birds in the palmetto and blackjack country. The shooting is about part way between the open shots afforded on a plantation hunt and the dense cover gunning in the Ozark-like country.

The dogs are let out of their crates in the back of the specially rigged four-wheel-drive vehicle. The hunters sit up high above the cab on seats and the driver follows the dogs cross country.

When the dogs find a covey and point, the vehicle is stopped, the hunters climb down, load up, and with the handler walk in to kick out the birds in front of the dogs. After the shot birds are gathered up, the singles are worked for a time, all hands walking. Then it's back to the vehicle and cross-country once more.

Because the quail, like the pheasant in the North, is a bird of agricultural lands it adapts well to artificial propagation, pen-rearing and stocking. And as more private lands are posted against trespass, both North and South, much of the quail shooting which future hunters will enjoy will come on game preserves, just as is the case with pheasant. At the present time some liberated quail are hard to tell from wild birds, but others are poor flyers and prefer running to flushing.

With the exception of the old bugaboo, wind, about the only concern for weather you'll probably have is that which involves your own comfort or lack of it. This will vary from section to section across the country.

In the South you may find yourself bird hunting in a tee-shirt in hot, dry cover, or bundled up against real cold late in the season in the north. When it is bitter cold, your pointing dog will probably have trouble locating quail, bunched up, deep in cover. However, by using Labrador retrievers and carefully working brushy draws where the birds would normally have been warm, secure and undisturbed, I have shot quail in Wisconsin when it was 5° below zero.

I like hunting in a warm drizzle or light rain. The cover is wet and you quickly get that way, too. But birds are on the move, there aren't many other hunters out and dogs work well. A cold rain or a downpour is something else again. But some of the best dog work and quail shooting I've enjoyed has come on drippy days in the oil fields of southeast Illinois and around the "tiff diggin's" (a mining operation) in central Missouri.

I also like overcast and threatening days with a little breeze and just the hint of some trouble in the air. It means birds will be out on the edge and fields probably right through the days and this is where a pointer is at his best.

I'm sorry I can't be more incisive and tell you to do this, there, at a certain time and you'll get a potful of birds. That just wouldn't be quail hunting. The real secret to successful quail hunting is a good dog or dogs and that discussion is reserved for another chapter.

Perhaps because I have been caught up in the mood of quail hunting as this is being written, you'll find this chapter rather rambling and casual. So let's leave the lackadaisical behind and get down to brass tacks. What kind of gun and load for quail hunting?

QUAIL GUNS AND LOADS

The covey rise was a blur and a whir—eleven pair of wings beating frantically to get the birds clear of the palmetto and out through the blackjack oak.

Picking the easiest straightaway bird, I touched off and saw two birds fall as a second bird came out of nowhere to cross the flight line of the bird I was concentrating on. A bird on my right had just reached altitude when I swung and dropped him, and out of the corner of my eye the bird to the left seemed still within range. He was, barely. For he dropped to the ground, not stone dead but a cripple easily recovered by the dog.

Now there are any number of good friends of mine who, without the slightest bit of encouragement, will willingly testify that "when Duffey gets four birds with three shots he might have got a lucky pellet into one, but the others died of heart attacks."

But they weren't there to enlighten my companions of the day in regard to my actual shooting ability. I have often been elated if I could take a pair of birds on a covey rise, although I always tried to give the impression that it was the usual thing and only a lack of ammo in the gun prevented me from wiping out the whole covey.

I'd like to be able to inform you modestly that since admittedly I'm not that good a shot, I have managed to select the world's best quail gun—one that never misses. But alas, much as I like the gun, I have missed before and will again with this and other smoothbores.

A quail shooter's gun should be as familiar to him as his forefinger and point just like it. Although after a time a good bobwhite shooter gains poise, on a covey rise the first moves are instinctive and there is no time for debate or deliberation. Quail are chopped down, in quick, decisive strokes, not smoothly tracked, swung through and folded as with pheasants.

So what kind of gun and load does this best? On that day I was shooting a Remington 870 pump gun, in 20 gauge with a 26-inch, ventilated-rib barrel, skeet boring. I have killed, and missed, quail with quite a variety of other guns.

There used to be a time when no real "sportsman" would gun upland birds with anything except a double barrel. But whatever the merits of the argument for double guns may be, it it readily apparent that not many hunters use them.

Cost may be a factor. Could be more poor folks are hunting quail today. But practicality enters in too. No longer have the doubles the only corner on the market when it comes to a light, fast-handling gun. Today's gun makers have put some little beauties on the market in autoloading and pump models.

So through sheer weight of numbers a man no longer has to have an inferiority complex about shooting a 3- to 5-shot pump or autoloader at quail, in preference to a double. In fact the generation gap is pretty clear when it comes to guns and maybe in another twenty-five years pump guns will be a thing of the past.

Just look around you. The grandfatherly types most frequently display side-by-side doubles. Their sons, if they shoot a double, seem to favor the superimposed but often carry a pump and quite a few boast autoloaders. My generation, when it comes to guns, is a mixed-up one. But the next generation, young man and boy, is autoloader armed.

So actually gun style is of little importance, except to say that everyone should have a gun that can be fired more than once without loading. It's the handling qualities that are important. Quite frankly, very often that's nothing more than what a man gets used to.

What about gauge? That's not too important either. A reasonably good shot can really work quail over with a .410 bore or 28-gauge. These birds get up close. If you are quick reacting you may be dropping the first bird on a rise less than ten yards from you. Because it is a small bird, a quail that makes it out thirty-five to forty yards from the gun presents a long, difficult shot and deserves to get off free.

However, you're lugging around a lot of extra weight and someone may sneer at your shooting ability if you regularly gun quail with a 12-gauge. If that's your only gun, fine. But if there is an ideal gauge for quail shooting it is the 20.

What about choke? Now we reach half of the meat of the matter. No matter what style or gauge from twenty to twelve, get a shotgun with an open boring. I think .410's and 28's should be bored modified in order to concentrate their light loads more and either kill cleanly or miss.

Cylinder bore is the most open boring you can get. It may be a bit too open for some, particularly an older, or slower-reacting shooter. But in any event it is more useful and appropriate than a full choke. Using a double barrel on quail, the fast gun-handler can utilize cylinder in the first barrel and improved cylinder in the second.

So the recommendation is a skeet or improved-cylinder boring. A good fast shot will get his close bird with it, still have enough oomph to reach for the second or even third. The slower reacting shooter who takes some time to get on that first bird will have an ideal pattern for it—and he can seldom get on a second bird anyway unless it's a late riser from a scattered covey.

Did I forget about loads? Not hardly. That's the second important item on the quail load agenda. On this matter I'm strongly with the consensus that advocates without equivocation the low brass, No. 8 shot is about as effective a load as you can loose at a bobwhite.

Those skeet and trap loads will give you a very uniform pattern and all the lead you need to effectively chop down quail. But if you're a high brass addict and don't mind spending the money I suppose there's no reason you can't bang away with a load of three and three quarter drams, an ounce and a quarter of seven and one-half shot (using 12 gauge as the scale). But that one-and-an-eighth ounces a 12-gauge trap load contains is more than enough.

After all, there's no problem killing with seven eighths of an ounce of No. 8's in a 20-bore and the one-ounce load is really deadly. If you really want to fling out a cloud of fine shot, you now can find high-brass loads of No. 9 shot. They're murder—on birds and on your teeth when you are feasting on your well-gotten game.

Your quail gun and loads will be nearly like or identical to the scattergun and shells you'll find most effective on ruffed grouse and woodcock. So if you're a Yankee who heads south for some different shooting or a Rebel who wants to sample what the north has to offer, you won't be embarrassed and you'll kill your share of birds if you take your favorite gun with you.

QUAIL SHOOTING

"How many'd you get?"

"Well, I got one down over here on the right and the dog's picking up my first bird out there in front now."

"Your bird! Don't tell me I'm shooting with some no-account bird claimer. I shot that bird the dog's got in his mouth."

Among strangers the above conversation could presage a bitter argument. But no sensible man shoots quail with strangers or with anyone whose character he hasn't sized up pretty well and found to his liking.

For quail shooting is often done in company and one of the more common things that can happen is for two experienced quail shots to each pick the easy bird out of the confusion of a covey rise, fire at it, see it drop and then swing to the birds going out their respective sides. Neither may hear the other's gun go off if their timing is identical.

The man who has shot a lot of birds knows this can happen and will get into jocular debates with his shooting partner about who really killed that bird, knowing full well that both probably centered on it. The neophyte shooter may find himself getting no shots while birds drop all around him, or else touching off at an already hit bird just a fraction after the bird's real killer has fired and winds up claiming a bird which, if he hit it at all, was already dead in the air.

Shooting bobwhites calls for concentration, precision shooting and teamwork. For this reason, I don't like to walk in past a dog with more than one other shooter, although I have hunted in parties of three and four when it couldn't be avoided. As a rule, two experienced shooters will drop just as many birds out of a covey rise by shooting the covey properly as will a handful of shooters each jockeying for position and frequently doubling on the same birds.

As pointed out at the start of this chapter, even then doubling can easily occur when both shooters start working from the center of the covey on out. But then it gets to be fun to see who can out-talk the other.

Quail shooting is close-range work and the birds must be cut down quickly before they get out of range. Therefore, as in ruffed-grouse shooting, forget about lead. If you have to consciously lead a bird, chances are good he's too far out for your open-bored pattern to do much good. Particularly on a covey rise, it also means that you have picked the wrong bird, if this is your first shot. Singles are a little different.

Two important things to remember were mentioned in the earlier chapter on quail hunting, but I repeat them here. Pick an individual bird. Don't flock-shoot. Keep your eyes up and looking ahead of the dog as you move in. Don't look at the ground.

Two hunters should walk in past the dog side by side. Then they won't interfere with each other or endanger each other. The birds will generally go out and away from you. If they should fly back over your heads, if you are on the left, turn to the left as you swing around, if on the right spin to the right—always the outside—so you don't swing a gun through your partner.

It's easier to describe how to kill almost any other bird. There are just no instructions that can be given to tell a man how to collect himself and precisely chop down two or three birds when a flock of half a dozen to two dozen explodes from underfoot.

You will learn this virtually instinctive shooting only by doing. I'd hazard a guess that just as most good waterfowl shots can down pheasants with regularity, a good ruffed grouse or woodcock shot will be able to hit quail with a little practice.

There is one complication, however. Quail are about the flattest-flying birds you will encounter. Birds usually get up a bit higher on covey rises and straggler birds that get out after the main body is on its way may lift a bit. But single birds almost invariably flash out there at grass cutting height. I think this is what throws a lot of shooters and causes some of the inexplicable misses that are chalked up on singles. If you miss the first shot at the single bird, you may also have to throw in a bit of conscious lead on your follow-up shot, because they get out and away *fast*. You get the impression that you are shooting down at the bird and this is a tough shot.

If you want to be polite in singles shooting, you can take turns with your partner or hold up until you see what slight or sharp angle the bird is taking and then let your partner shoot if it is to his side. But shooting single quail makes for a great contest between two friendly shooters. Generally the bird is an almost straightaway shot and fair game for either shooter. The fun is seeing who can get on the bird quickest and drop it out from under his partner.

But if hurrying a shot bothers you, don't engage in this sport. Your bird score will be pretty low.

4

A Sporty Migrant
THE WOODCOCK

LIKE an oak leaf in an updraft, the cinnamon-colored, grotesque little bird made it to the top of the thick clump of tag alders along the creek bank. There it was intercepted by a charge of fine shot. It fell—softly—and once on the ground could not have been detected except by the keen nose of the questing spaniel that had put the bird into flight.

Although about half a million of these transformed shore birds are killed in this manner each year, the woodcock remains the mystery bird of the uplands. Wildlife researchers pay it scant attention, many hunters cannot identify it, others ignore it and those who hunt woodcock form their own speculations and ideas about the bird's comings and goings.

This little brown bird, with black and white trim, is the only migrant among our upland bird species. Because he is a migrant, and ornithologists lump *Philohela minor* with snipe and sandpipers, some might argue that the woodcock has no more place in a book about upland bird hunting than does the mourning dove. But woodcock are hunted and shot in the same way as the chicken-like birds which comprise most of our upland species. Most frequently, they are shot in conjunction with ruffed grouse or are incidental to a ruffed-grouse hunt, for these two birds often frequent the same covert.

The Creator of birds didn't pass out favors lavishly when He designed the woodcock. On the ground or in the air he resembles an alderman who has dined too well, too often. Chunky and neck-less, his ears are set just below his prominent, round eyes. The upper portion of his long bill is jointed and can work independently of the lower.

This bill enables him to probe soft soil in search of earthworms and minute crustacean morsels, grasp them and extract them from the ground. Because he feeds little, if at all, on anything but earth-bound animal life, his life is governed by the weather; for when the ground is frozen he cannot probe it.

Not much larger than a bobwhite quail, even when fat in the fall, a woodcock that reaches half a pound in weight is a real buster. Females generally run larger than males. Females also sport longer bills than the males. A rule of thumb, if you're interested in sex differentiation, is that if the upper portion of the bill measures 2½ inches or less the bird is male. There is some overlap, however, both in bill length and body weight. The outermost primary wing feather on the females is usually broader, but such measurements are cutting it pretty fine for a hunter. In flight there is no way to tell a cock from a hen bird.

You are sure to encounter reputable citizens who hunt woodcock and claim they can tell "flight" birds from locals. "Flight" birds, they say, are always larger. Could be. But I don't believe it and you don't have to.

More than likely the kill of "flight" birds simply was made up mostly of females, along with the added factor of some additional fat that woodcock lard up with late in the season. Local birds, in the same region, of the same sex, are probably comparable in size.

However, you can logically conclude that the "flight is on" if cover that held good numbers of woodcock the day before is deserted the following day, and/or good woodcock country that was barren of birds the previous day is loaded with the little twisters today.

Because they migrate at night and would be perfectly content to remain unobtrusively in thick coverts through the day unless disturbed by man and dog, the woodcock retains an air of mystery. Often, when seen by man, it's in the bad light of early morn or late evening and the bird is not identified.

Many a casual hunter has fired several times at this strange bird, sometimes honestly believing it was a grouse flush. But frequent misses, as the erratic flight pattern eludes the shot charge, will cause him to refuse to "waste shells on those damn funny-lookin' birds."

The hunter who happens to bag only an occasional woodcock may misidentify it as a jacksnipe (Wilson's snipe). But except for the long bill there is little resemblance between the two birds. In contrast to the rich brown coloration of the woodcock, the jacksnipe is slatey in appearance and has green legs as opposed to the pinkish-orange of the woodcock's.

Nor are the flight patterns of the two birds similar. Both are erratic—but the woodcock's is fluttery on the rise and descent, but can be string-straight after the getaway, while the jacksnipe zig-zags once in the clear. Jacksnipe are more likely to frequent wet meadows, marsh edges and generally open lowlands.

If it were not for the chittering sound made by his wings as he gets into flight, the woodcock (who will sit tight until literally stepped upon by a hunter) could get up and away with the best of ghosts and spooks. He is actually slow to get underway, and the thing that makes him such a sporty and elusive target is the heavy cover he frequents and his inconsistent, dodging flight on the rise.

While a few woodcock are shot incidentally to quail hunting in the South, and vast numbers of the birds winter in Louisiana, the woodcock is primarily for the Northern hunter. The heaviest kills are recorded in states like Michigan, Wisconsin, New York, Maine, and New Jersey, and Canadian provinces like Nova Scotia, New Brunswick, Ontario and Quebec.

More often than not the hunter who successfully guns woodcock is also a ruffed-grouse hunter. A couple of partridge and two or three "timberdoodles," the woodcock's most common nickname, are one of the most common mixed bags for the Northeastern hunter.

Furthermore, when an upland hunter gets mixed up with a flight of woodcock it's "Katy bar the door." He'll get some of the fastest and trickiest shooting he can imagine, and once he's encountered this kind of hunting he's likely to forsake all others to pursue it. Woodcock hunters, although few in number, easily become fanatics.

During the middle two weeks in October in favorite haunts in my home state of Wisconsin, it is not unusual to have forty to fifty woodcock flushes in two to three hours while traversing forty to a hundred and sixty acres. This is fast shooting. While not high, the legal limit on the migratory woodcock is usually more generous than on local game. The past few years it has been five.

Even the most experienced woodcock shot will miss. And although I have had some lucky streaks, the day is well spent in terms of shells expended if I get a bird for every three to four shots, taking them as they come, pushed up by a spaniel or retriever trained to hunt like a spaniel. The first-time woodcock shooter may burn up a box of shells downing one or two. After such a performance, many quit in disgust. Others persevere to become ardent woodcock hunters and fine wing shots.

WOODCOCK-HUNTING TACTICS

Woodcock would be easier to find and simple to hit if they'd only hang around until the hard frosts and rains of late October strip the the foliage from the birch and aspen slopes, and make skeletons out of the tag alder, red osier and willow that clog the creek bottoms.

But impelled by ripples of cold weather, these warm-brown birds move out just about the time you can comfortably wear a wool shirt at midday and long-john underwear has become essential in the early morning hours.

Thus, if you are to pot some local birds before they pull out to be replaced by "flight birds" from the north, your hunting day should start just as soon as the state laws say it is legal to shoot. Then if you are lucky, wise in your selection of hunting site, and quick and accurate with a shotgun, perhaps you will have limited out by the time the heat of early autumn makes the tangled coverts a challenge to the endurance and tenacity of man and dog rather than a fun-filled recreational pursuit.

Furthermore, local birds are never present in the almost unbelievable numbers that show up when migrants have dropped into good cover. And while they will likely provide some hunting over a longer period of time before they decide to move out, it is best to work on them while they are moving. Being primarily nocturnal birds, they are still out feeding those first two hours on any nice morning.

So the knowledgeable woodcock hunter puts in his hunting stint before going to work, until that first glorious morning dawns. He then hits his favorite cover, and every twenty yards or so the dog gets a bird up. When he shoots and drops a bird, sometimes another flushes from the spot the shot bird fell as the dog goes in to retrieve. *A flight is in.*

By that time hard frost has nipped the leaves, but even though the ground is white with it in the early morning, by mid-morning the dripping brush has dried off and the day stays bright and crisp. Birds tarry, for the ground still accepts their probing bills. When they leave, others replace them. For ten days to two weeks in mid-October, every woodcock hunter knows for certain that he has died and gone to heaven, for while it lasts, there is no better or faster shooting offered on the North American continent. In many coverts the shooting is further spiced by frequent cracks at ruffed grouse, an occasional flush of a ringneck rooster or the rippled water rise of a puddle duck surprised on a backwater or slough.

Then, when the still ponds are rimmed with ice in the morning or skimmed over and the cover has been opened by sharp north winds and rain (now sleety and cold, rather than slow and comforting as it was earlier), only a late straggler or two surprises the hunter who must go out "just one more time."

Thus, physically and psychologically, the woodcock hunter passes through three stages during the three to five weeks that provide birds to shoot during the open season.

At the season's start, after the initial anticipation has worn off, he settles down to a trance-like job of performing a chore. It takes blood, sweat and tears to bag woodcock early in the season. Branches raise welts on a man's face, and if he neglects to wear shooting glasses, a sharp twig in the eye is a real hazard. Briars and thorns tear the skin on hands and draw blood, and unless the hunter's legs are protected by double-faced pants, they will be polka-dotted and diagonaled by the jabs and slashes of brambles.

Mornings in early autumn are muggy and the hunter will sweat as he swats mosquitoes. He will cry in anguish and frustration as a bird slips through a screen of dense green foliage too heavy to shoot through or when the effective portion of his well-directed shot charge is absorbed by a thicket or a tree trunk.

But the only way the sportsman can know when the flights start coming in is by being in the coverts for at least an hour or so every day, or at least two or three mornings a week. Then, when the flight birds start piling in it's time to "phone in sick." Planning your time off in advance is a bit unpredictable, and you may get stung. However, most years in latitudes where I do most of my wood-cocking (Wisconsin) you can figure the best shooting will occur sometime between the 7th and 21st of October.

Before that, you *must* hunt hard, under frustrating conditions, to shoot local birds. After that, the shooting tails off and the latest I've ever shot a straggler woodcock in northeastern or central Wisconsin was November 17. Unless there's unusually mild weather, there's little woodcock shooting to be had after the first week in November. Early hard freezes may push birds through and shorten the pro-ductive hunting time.

These little rascals can be unpredictable too. Many years ago when my son, Mike, was still shorter than I, we planned a mid-October trip for woodcock some distance west of our home with the late Milo Mabie, a Neillsville, Wisconsin sportsman. Milo made a living barbering when the woodcock season wasn't open but couldn't be counted on to shear you in October. He hunted every morning for two to four hours and was easily enticed out on an afternoon. As a result, Milo knew more about where the woodcock were and when they ought to be there than anyone I know but freely admitted they frequently fooled him as to location. Despite bagging thousands he got a kick out of missing and his self-derisive whoop could be heard along the Jackson and Clark county creek bottoms when one of the little tantalizers slipped away from his shot pattern.

On the day I'm thinking of, we were leaving the house about 5 A.M. when the phone rang. Milo was sick and couldn't make the hunt. I make it a rule that when a man shows me his best hunting country, I never return to it unless I'm with him. (The surest way to get good hunting country over-populated with humans and shot out is to take your friends to those spots. So I refuse to pull on any-one else the stunt of going back with a carload of other hunters on another day.)

I sure had a disappointed youngster on my hands, and I was all primed to go, too. The frost was thick on everything, not just in the low spots. "Maybe that cold weather brought some ducks in," I said to Mike. "Let's go see if we can jump a few off the potholes out at the land and then we'll head for a spot where I've missed a few partridge. I usually run into some woodcock there."

But the freeze was hard enough to have put more than just a skim of ice on the potholes and not an orange-footed mallard did we see. "Not much chance of any woodcock being in now," I informed Mike. "But let's give our pointer pup a little work so the day won't be wasted."

It doesn't take many hunting trips to disillusion a boy about the infallibility of his father. But this time, I was happy to be wrong. The upshot was that in a short morning's hunt in two coverts within ten miles of my home we had fifty-odd woodcock flushes, spiced up by half a dozen ruffed grouse. We "broke" a brand-new woodcock dog in one day.

For what little it's worth, my explanation is that while the cold had probably moved the local birds out (I say local because prior to that day the cover had held only scattered birds) a flight of tired birds had moved in from the north during the night and settled in for a rest.

That Sunday night the phone rang. It was Bob Skoronski, a tackle and offensive captain of the Green Bay Packers football team. I've had the pleasure of frequently hunting with these gridiron gentlemen and have trained dogs for several of them. Bob and the rest of the team had just gotten into Green Bay by plane after a game away from home. Monday was their usual day off.

"Where we going tomorrow?" Bob asked. That year we had more or less a standing date to hunt together on Mondays. Although a Connecticut native, Bob had bagged his first woodcock earlier that year while on a hunt with Milo Mabie and me, and had quickly become a convert. "We won't have much time, though," he added. "The old man (Coach Vince Lombardi) has scheduled a skull session."

Warning him that I was guaranteeing nothing, I told him what Mike and I had run into. "Those two pieces of cover are only about forty acres each, depending upon how much time you've got, we can cover one or both of them well and they're close to home. But the birds may have pulled out overnight."

This time again I was lucky. There was just over an hour of legal hunting time remaining when I let a Springer spaniel and a Labrador retriever out of their dog crates in the back of the four-wheel-drive Scout, parked square in the middle of the hunting cover. Bob had brought along a couple of other Lombardi-era interior linemen, Chuck Voss and Ken Iman. But even for four hunters —really too large a party for any upland hunt—forty-odd woodcock in the air in an hour can burn up a lot of ammo.

We never left the first covert. So what does a place that seems to offer everything to woodcock look like? The center of the first cover was an abandoned farm clearing, now grown up into high grass clumps interspersed with young white pines that had been seeded naturally from the few the loggers had missed years before. Surrounding this clearing was a dense growth of tag alder and red osier brush. While fighting our way through the brush we'd encounter little clearings of high ground, some of them supporting a few stunted poplar trees.

Sand ridges, on which birch, scrub oak, poplar and occasionally a large pine, stuck out above the cold bottom lowlands. These lowlands were drained into a huge marshland that bordered the Wolf River by creek-like ditches from an abandoned drainage project. Woodcock were working the clearing and island edges and the bottom of the ridge slopes adjacent to bog and ditch.

The second site, which we didn't reach that day, was on the opposite side of the river and similar in topography and vegetation. Instead of ditches, however, a free flowing stream drained the boglands which are treacherously soft. Birds were in the brushy bog edges.

The country I've hunted with Milo Mabie, which lies about a hundred miles to the west of my home, is very similar—the bottomlands of a fast moving stream, or lowlands dotted with high ground and laced by a stream or wet ditch.

If when rambling cross country you run into a young pine plantation, or a stump-strewn, cut-over area, don't pass it up. You are likely to find woodcock on the forest floor under the pines or among the dead ferns in the logged-over clearings.

But good-looking cover isn't a sure guarantee of woodcock shooting, unfortunately. For example, one of my favorite "partridge roads" goes straight for three miles through some of the most ideal woodcock and ruffed-grouse cover you'd hope to see.

This is always a sure bet for ruffed grouse early in the morning, but I have shot only a few straggler woodcock off the always-wet ditches that border this road. The migrant birds, I think, sometimes simply fail to discover good, new territory because they usually utilize the familiar places; or some important factor may be lacking.

At the end of the road, however, lies a forty-acre piece of low ground, containing some stunted second-growth hardwood and some old birch and poplar, red osier and even some stands of canary grass. It is bordered on three sides by wet ditches. Particularly in a dry year, this always contains birds. Part of it is also an abandoned farmsite.

Rainfall may also be a factor in determining where you'll find birds. If the lowlands are too wet, apparently the birds cannot feed. Conversely, in very dry years some spots will hold birds that did not have any in previous years, because the soil, though now walkable rather than wadeable, remains damp, and moisture (if it is not excessive) makes earthworms and minute organisms available for the birds.

It's been my observation that seldom will you find woodcock near stagnant water. The border of a stream is much more productive, and drainage ditches will do.

Despite the fact that a lot of woodcock are killed in highly urbanized and heavily farmed states, just like the ruffed grouse, it is a wilderness bird in that it prefers so-called "wild lands" to agricultural country.

However, in some parts of the country a common agricultural practice appears to be an aid to woodcock hunting. Very often, normal plant succession will take over a covert to the point where it is simply too thick for woodcock. During dry years it is common practice for dairy farmers to turn young stock into the lowlands to glean whatever forage is available there. When not overdone, pasturing stock in these near-swampy areas not only opens it up for woodcock, but results in trails, made by the livestock, which allow easier walking and more open gunning for the hunter.

Woodcock should be hunted with a dog. Woodcock will sit tight to a point, rather than flushing wild like a ruffed grouse or running like a pheasant. Thus they are a wonderful bird for the fanciers of pointing dogs, if the cover is broken enough and the dog a close enough hunter so he can be kept track of.

Woodcock apparently leave a strong scent, and they do move about—although about the only time a man sees them is when they are standing still on the ground or are up in the air. Flushing dogs, like spaniels and retrievers, also do well. Many a dog who is an otherwise fine bird-fetcher, however, refuses to retrieve woodcock. We'll go into more detail in the dog section.

Woodcock can also be hunted without a dog, if the hunter proceeds very slowly, stopping often; but so wonderfully camouflaged are these birds, that they are even more adept than grouse at holding tight and letting the hunter walk by them undetected. If a man looks hard and close, sometimes he can spot a sitting woodcock, usually by the shine of its prominent eye. However, it is generally a slow and unrewarding process, and one can properly cover five times the territory in half the time with a dog.

The timberdoodle is also a fine bird to utilize in introducing a youngster to the art of wing shooting. The bird is not fast, despite its elusiveness; it gets up close to the gun, and you can usually get enough of them into the air to keep a youngster keen by providing legitimate shots.

When woodcock flush they do not fly far, as a rule. If you miss or do not get off a shot, follow the line of flight and mark where the bird comes down. Then hunt toward him (often putting up other birds in the process) and kick him out again.

Because they often drop down suddenly to end their flight, thus giving the shooter the impression that he's scored a hit, more than one hunter has been caught unprepared when he sent his dog to fetch, or walked in to pick up a "dead bird," only to have a perfectly healthy specimen flit out of the cover and disappear.

However, when you're pretty sure you have hit a bird, don't give up the search for it just because you see a bird rise from the spot you'd marked as the fall. When flights are in, very often a dead bird will drop almost on top of another live bird. Encourage your dog to hunt out the area of your marked fall so you waste no game.

Every gourmet will tell you that woodcock are a real table delicacy. I'm going to tell you different. I have eaten woodcock prepared by at least a dozen different cooks and I still don't like to eat them. They rank at the absolute bottom of my personal "game birds I like to eat" totem pole.

I will concede that if wild duck is one of your favorite table staples, you will probably rate woodcock higher than I do. If so, as a gift, I give you all I can shoot. I like beef, calf, venison and chicken liver. But I don't appreciate a liverish taste in birds and that's what woodcock have.

What do I do with my birds? I'm fortunate in having friends with gourmet appetites but no interest in hunting. They'll even dress the birds. Sometimes I very slyly con a hunting partner into taking a limit of woodcock in exchange for the lone partridge he shot. If I'm stuck with a bagful of woodcock, as a last desperate measure I turn the dressed birds over to my wife who cuts the breasts up in small pieces and mixes them with the meat of other game birds to add tang to casserole and meat-pie-type dishes.

This is just to let you know that if you've been keeping it a deep, dark secret that you like woodcock to shoot but can forgo eating them, there's no need to be ashamed or pretend otherwise. You've got a lot of company.

WOODCOCK GUNS AND LOADS

When it comes to guns or loads for woodcock shooting there isn't a lot to be said that hasn't already been covered in the quail and ruffed-grouse sections. Any gun and load with which you can satisfactorily kill bobwhite and partridge is adequate, if not ideal, for woodcock shooting. In other words, you want a short-barreled, open-choked gun, stuffed with light field-loads of 8's or 9's.

If you are planning to concentrate on woodcock and want a special gun for it, remember that you cannot find a gun with too open a choke for woodcock shooting and that nothing larger than a .410 is too small. The more you hunt woodcock, the more likely you are to realize this. For example, my previously mentioned woodcock-shooting buddy, Milo Mabie, had his favorite "bird gun" (a Fox Model B, 20-gauge side-by-side) opened up by a gunsmith from its original improved-cylinder and modified borings. The first barrel is now chokeless, the "tight" barrel, improved cylinder.

Much of the woodcock's reputation as an extremely difficult bird to hit stems from the fact that a large percentage of hunters on the North American continent has always preferred just the opposite type of gun. Partly this is the result of the old American axiom that if a certain portion of something (it could be milk, money or cigarettes, among other things) is either good for you or enjoyable, more of the same should be even better.

But there's more to it than this. Midwestern and Western pheasant and prairie-grouse hunters and all waterfowl hunters are partial to "long shootin'" smokepoles, and rightly so. These game birds require tightly choked smoothbores and a substantial charge of shot if the hunter is to wind up satisfied rather than frustrated. Furthermore, when selling a gun, any salesman who can tout a really "hard hitting" shotgun has a lot going for him.

Now, most hunters come to savor the joys of woodcock shooting rather late in life. I don't mean to imply that it's an old man's game; the point is, the vast majority start out on some other game bird. If woodcock were an important bird, sportwise, in the South, there'd be no problem. Quail guns and loads are A-1 for woodcock.

But it happens that they are most avidly pursued farther north, where chances are good the sportsman has already selected a gun for pheasant or waterfowl shooting. The chances are also good that this gun will be a pump- or autoloading 12-gauge with a 28- to 32-inch full-choke barrel. This happens to be just about the worst sort of instrument one can lug around in the tag alder tangles.

Furthermore, the bulk of yesterday's and today's hunters either own only a single shotgun, or else have the most confidence in the one gun in their collection that they shoot the most. And, by figuring that they'll be making more waterfowl and pheasant hunting trips than they will jaunts for woodcock, they stick with the full choke.

I can't argue with this reasoning. But let me suggest that, if you are to get any enjoyment and any fit-for-the-table birds on a woodcock hunt, you fit out your "long gun" with screw in changeable choke tubes or compensators, buy a second 24-26 inch barrel, bored skeet, cylinder or improved cylinder (or a second set of barrels, if your gun is a twin-tube), or use only special shells called "spreader" or "brush" loads.

But yes, Virginia, there is an "ideal" woodcock gun—if you want to spend the money for it and if you'll shoot it enough to get used to it.

The double barrel, whether side-by-side or over-and-under, is ideally suited for woodcock shooting. Practically all decent doubles are expensive, but no other gun has quite the balance and handling qualities they do. You may also argue that they lack firepower. But in woodcock shooting, so seldom do you need more than two shots at a time that it isn't even worth considering. Furthermore, when the flights are in, since this is a sport shooting game rather than a pot-filling contest, you can be assured that there will be plenty of other shooting opportunities should you miss twice. Just grin and give the little rascal his due for successfully eluding you.

Who knows? You may well find that you get more actual shooting at birds on a single woodcock jaunt than you do during your several hunts for pheasant and decide that the woodcock gun is the one you really want to learn to shoot well.

WOODCOCK SHOOTING

Ever shot fish in a barrel? Neither have I, nor have I ever encountered anyone who has. But it is an interesting expression and it connotes easy shooting.

If a "fish-in-a-barrel" shoot appeals to you, don't try woodcock. These baffling little birds of the boondocks have been causing hunters to cuss for as many years as men have tried to down them with a load of fine shot.

It has to be the woodcock's unpredictable and erratic flight that can send otherwise sane gunners to the brink. This flight has been described variously and colorfully by penmen with more imagination than I.

But the classic description of the flight of these artful dodgers came from the lips of one Carl Erskine, former Brooklyn-Los Angeles Dodger pitcher, several decades ago when we were hunting the little long-bills along the Flambeau River in northern Wisconsin.

Erskine, who was on his first woodcock hunt, was an experienced shotgunner, having done his share of quail shooting in his home state of Indiana. So it didn't take long for him to start scoring respectably on the timberdoodles my brace of Labrador retrievers put out for him.

But after he had watched the first three corkscrew off through the still heavy foliage he lowered his little 28-gauge and shook his head in admiration. "Darned if those little dudes don't hang up there just like Hoyt Wilhelm's knuckle ball," he said. And many a hunter will add, "Just as hard to hit, too."

In a way, I have to go along with the "tough-to-hit" evaluation, large'y because, like you, I'm often in need of an excuse to explain some misses. But woodcock really aren't—or at least they shouldn't be—hard birds to center a pattern on. But as with no other bird, a man's shooting will be "streaky"—deadly one day, unbelievably inept the next.

Unawed by the woodcock's reputation, Erskine's companion on that particular hunting trip, Bob Bauman, a former pro gridder, had run up some "impossible" string, such as eight for eight, on a mixed woodcock and ruffed-grouse bag. But that was one trip. Maybe he hasn't gotten his comeuppance yet, but I'll bet he has.

At one time, relatively early in my career as a shooter of woodcock and partridge, I figured I had found the formula that was going to make gunning these birds as boringly repetitious as powdering the high-house, station-7 bird on a skeet field. Hunting with Tony Jelich, a game warden buddy out of Solon Springs, Wisconsin, I hammered down a bag limit (which, combining ruffed grouse and woodcock, was eight or ten birds, I disremember which) missing only once. And the cover was brutal.

That's when I should have quit and written a book on how to hit those tricky birds. But I didn't. The next day found me in another hot woodcock covert, about seventy miles to the east. Fortunately I was alone, so I wouldn't really have to confess this— but the first seven birds that twisted up out of those tag alders never lost a feather, and most of them I shot at twice!

But that's what I mean about "streaky" shooting. Gunners sometimes have those days. Ordinarily, you are justified if you are skeptical of a pheasant or quail shooter who is missing shot after shot and still trying to convince you that he's usually the grim reaper when it comes to wiping out the shootable bird population. Just don't be too quick to doubt the word of a bedeviled-by-misses woodcock shooter. He may be an honest man.

So, while it ain't easy to hit woodcock, you will greatly increase your score if you'll just take it easy. A great number of misses come because a bunch of half-cocked reflexes belonging to a startled hunter go off prematurely.

There is an old axiom: One shot, dead bird. Two shots, maybe Three shots, still flying. To some extent this applies to woodcock as well as other game birds. But it just could be that almost as many woodcock are killed with the second shot as with the first. No bird gets up closer than the timberdoodle, whether walked up, pointed by a dog or flushed by a dog.

Despite the difficult cover the woodcock is found in, even the slowest-reacting hunter can get off a second shot at the bird. And for Hair-trigger Harry, he's already with his second shot before the bird gets to where it should have been for his first shot.

Not only does the woodcock get up close to the gun but while he's going somewhere (you'd never guess where from his rising, twisting flight) he's not going there very fast.

Now, I'm not suggesting you stand around, blow your nose and clean your glasses while you're waiting for him to get out a little ways. That slow he ain't, and the cover is thick. You have to cover him quickly if you are going to score. But be deliberately fast, not palpitatingly rapid. And, as with ruffed grouse, forget all that jazz about lead. Poke that gun barrel out there and hope.

There is no predicting which direction a flushed woodcock will take. Generally it will be away from you. But when the bird is being worked by a flushing dog, and is concerned with eluding dog, not man, he may come right at you. Several times a year I actually hit a woodcock's body or have his wing brush my gun barrel as I bring it up.

This just shows you how rattled a man can get. *That kind of incomer is no shot.* When a woodcock pulls that stunt on you, turn in the direction of his flight and after he passes over you, take him going away.

Much has been said about the bird's corkscrew-like flight pattern, which contributes to misses as he zigs while you zag. But if you flush him along trails or tote roads, or out of a thicket on a bog edge, upon reaching altitude (seldom higher than the tops of whatever he's getting out of) he will bore off, straight as a string, providing a straightaway shot. If he's twenty yards or more away from you this will be a shot at a descending bird, so figure accordingly.

If you shoot and miss the first shot, if you don't anticipate a change-up you'll miss the second time. For that laggardly bird that seemed to hang in the air can jet along, when he hears the pellets swishing around him.

A woodcock hunter's gun is going to get a bit beat-up. Not only because he thrusts through tangles with it but because he may have to bang it through the brush as he mounts and swings it.

Don't let branches deter you. Get that gun up and poke at that bird. Sure, brush is going to hamper your swing, but swing anyway. (Once in a while you'll hit something you can't swing through, like a sapling or a tree trunk. It's a jolting experience, but gun barrels are pretty hard to bend.)

Is there a simple shot while woodcocking? I think so. Like everything else, it depends upon circumstances. In the right cover, you and your shooting partner can hike your averages by using a flushing dog like a spaniel or any dog trained to hunt in this manner:

Gunners walk down each side of a tag-alder-covered stream bank, or position themselves as they work along a ridge bordering a bog edge, keeping as clear of the brush as possible. The dog is sent down into the tangle. He has to be well trained and know what he's doing—often you will not be able to see the dog. But you will hear the peculiar sound of a flushed woodcock, and spot him as he tops the cover.

Woodcock like to rise to the top of low cover they frequent before boring off or slanting back in. Your vision is going to be as unobscured, and your gun swing as unimpeded, as at any time in woodcocking. As the bird tops the cover he will hang there for an instant. That's when you pop him.

Real simple, ain't it? Well, frankly, I'm glad it isn't. And about the time you get real cocky and start thinking it is, start taking a "shell count."

This consists of carefully counting the shells you start out with on the hunt—no chiseling, 'cause it's easy, in the excitement of being mixed up in a flight, to forget you dug into that second box of shells when you stopped at the car. Then compare how many you've used to the number of birds in your game pocket.

This can have a sobering effect on the most intoxicated-with-success woodcock hunter. So don't do any shell counting until you've been on a real binge.

5
Gambler's Game Bird
THE HUNGARIAN PARTRIDGE

A BIRD for big country, the Hungarian partridge in some instances has filled the void left by the decline of the prairie grouse, but rates as probably one of the least discussed, yet most cussed, of our upland game birds.

Like the pheasant, the Hun (known in Europe as the European gray partridge) is an import. And like the big Oriental rascal, the Hungarian has some pretty perverse habits, like running rather than sitting tight to a pointing dog, zig-zagging and doubling back behind hunters, and flushing wild.

"Hunkies" are not what might be called commonly hunted birds, even in the states and provinces where they are fairly abundant. Going under the Latin designation of *Perdix perdix*, the birds picked up their common name in this country because they are common on the plains of Hungary and most of our original importations came from that country.

Hungarians were liberated in the United States around the turn of the twentieth century and tried in the Eastern and Southern states as well as elsewhere in the nation, but they seemed to "take" only in some of the far-western states, in the upper Mississippi valley and the Canadian provinces of Manitoba, Saskatchewan and Alberta.

In some states their range has overlapped that of the pheasant, in others the prairie grouse (sharptail and prairie chicken), and maybe a dozen states have either extensive areas or scattered spots where there are shootable populations of Huns.

They took hold most vigorously in the wheat-growing provinces of the Canadian prairies and less extensively in such Western states as Idaho, Oregon, Montana, Washington and the Dakotas. But Midwestern states like Wisconsin and Minnesota also boast some of these birds.

There really is no reason to confuse Hungarian partridge with any other game bird. Weighing about three-quarters of a pound and about a foot long from beak to tail tip, it is a bird distinctly larger than a quail and smaller than a ruffed grouse.

Predominately gray, pastel in tone not unlike a mourning dove, the color blends to brownish on the back and in flight the bird may display an orangy or rusty tail. The sexes appear identical in flight but when in the hand the hunter can tell the gentlemen from the lady Hungarians by examining the breast and head. The cock has a dark brown, horseshoe-shaped mark on the lower breast; the mark is at best partial and often absent on the hen. The cock's head is a more solid brown color, while the head and neck of the hen tend toward gray.

However, excited hunters have been known to misidentify them as sharp-tailed grouse when they've been flushed from a bluff in the midst of some grain fields; and Northern hunters, not well acquainted with either bird, have referred to Hungarians as quail when they occasionally sighted them.

In their habits, though not in appearance, Huns seem to be an odd cross between pheasant and quail. They travel in groups led by an old bird, and, like coveys of quail, roost in a circle on the ground, heads pointing out.

Despite their flocking habits, they are, like the pheasant, frequently reluctant to hold for a dog; they'd give a pheasant plenty of competition in a foot race, and they like to take flight well out of gun range. And when a Hun flies he doesn't mess around with short hops. He'll go half a mile or more before dropping down, often flying right over or past good cover to alight in another open field.

This bird loves flat, open land. Hunters will most commonly find him right smack in the middle of a wheat-stubble field. He likes grain. Stubble fields of all kinds attract him, the bigger the better.

In some areas, like the flat country to east central Wisconsin along the Lake Michigan shoreline, where dairy rather than grain farming holds sway, large fields with a sprinkling of clover or grown-over with ragweed are good bets. The early fall may find the bird around fallow fields, for while they do like cultivated plains lands, they can do fairly well on fringe lands.

Masters of concealment, they can remain hidden, singly or in groups, in an open stubble field, a dusty corn row or on bare ground under a sparse ragweed and goldenrod wasteland.

A hardy bird that can withstand severe weather, making out on weeds, buds, pickings from the manured fields and other above-the-snow offerings, the Hun is not above venturing near farm buildings to pick up sustenance in a bad winter.

Sometimes the Hungarian inhabits the same country as the sharp-tailed grouse. However, since the sharpie likes the wilder grazing lands in preference to the more agricultural, and more and more lands are being turned to wheat, in many areas the Hun may well replace the native sharptail as a sought-after bird. Right now the hunter who hits the vast prairie-lands of Alberta, Saskatchewan and Manitoba will probably get in more Hun hunting than sharp-tail shooting.

Perhaps if some economic disaster should ever return those vistas of bright yellow stubble to grayish-green grasslands, interspersed with thickets of willow and aspen around potholes, it will be the sharptail's turn. But now, despite their perversity, let's go Hun hunting.

HUN-HUNTING TACTICS

We lay stretched out on the hill, in the shade of a small clump of yellow-leaved aspen with a breeze to dispel the unseasonable heat of an early October day in southern Saskatchewan, and our noon siesta seemed like the best idea since the discovery of the wheel.

We'd been hiking hard all morning and had been rewarded with a pretty good bag of sharp-tailed grouse. But with the sun beating down, temperatures had pushed into the low 80's by lunch time and a man could kill a willing dog by running him in this arid region.

So I watered Twist, my white and black Pointer bitch, and Briar, my German wirehaired Pointer, from the canteens in the station wagon. Then after we had a sandwich, Bill Brauer, a Fond du Lac, Wisconsin clothier and I lay back in the grass to nap and wait for the cool of late afternoon.

When I heard the first bird call, I thought maybe I was dreaming, being that close to sleep. Then I heard Bill stir. When I opened my eyes and turned my head he was up on one elbow. "You hear that?" he asked. I nodded. "Think it was a covey call?" I nodded again.

There below us, in the dry bottom of a brush-surrounded pothole which had been mowed of marsh hay, a covey of Hungarian partridge was assembling. We knew it must be the covey we had broken up as we were coming back into the car when the dogs, wrong-way to the hot wind that was scorching the countryside, bumped into and ran through the birds. All thoughts of sleep were gone.

Strangely enough, we'd had some trouble locating Huns, and actually had enjoyed better luck with sharptails thus far on the trip. Earlier in the morning Twist had snapped on a beautiful point and Briar backed, forty yards away from us in the midst of a stubble field. But as we'd hustled across the bright stubble the backing dog had sneaked past the statuesque Pointer and taken one step too many, and the birds had exploded. After devoting a few moments and choice expletives to making a Christian out of Briar we'd moved on, but never could relocate the covey.

So now it was hard for us to wait until we'd given those birds down in the bluff fifteen or twenty minutes to get together. By the time the calling finally stopped, we had our shotguns out of the station wagon. I let Twist out by herself. She was half-beat—the heat, with no water to wallow in, had taken its toll.

But the hot wind was coming towards us from the birds' assembly area. Her nose tested it and she made a trotting bee-line for the cover a good 150 yards away. Right at the edge nearest us she froze in mid-stride, her right hind leg held in the air.

By the time we'd gotten twenty yards from her, the leg went down and she took a couple of steps forward. I whoaed her and walked out in front while Bill got set but could produce no birds. Twist was then sent on. She pointed again, then moved off on her own volition as she worked around the fringe of cover. This time, knowing she was dealing with running birds, I gave her her head.

I don't like to see a good pointing dog work like this, but with running pheasants—or in this case running Huns—it sometimes has to be done. She walked on eggs for twenty-five yards, then locked up again. She held as I walked past her and thrashed around. No birds. I told her, "All right!" and she moved out with a sprightly dash, only to shut down abruptly and start egg-walking again.

She froze once more. I was getting disgusted by this time. "Dammit! Quit this pussy-footing. Either pin 'em or flush 'em." Twist flinched a bit at the shouting, took a couple tentative steps ahead and again stopped, but without the rigid intensity she'd displayed before. By now we were halfway around the pothole.

I barged in, knowing better than to vent my feelings by boosting her out of there, but reaching down to tap her on the head to send her out to make a positive relocation. Before I could touch her, however, the covey went up all around me. The dog and I were smack in the middle of it.

There must have been just under two dozen birds in this big Hun bevy. They scattered in every direction, although the main body went straight north.

I was happy I had the presence of mind to shoot the gun, even though nothing fell. But Bill had coolly cut down a pair of birds, and the dog got her reward anyway.

Now, Huns aren't always that hard for a dog to handle, and every now and then they'll even present an easy shot. But maybe you can see from that experience why the words "crafty" and "perverse" are fittingly applied to these slatey buzz-bombs.

You won't have your midday nap interrupted too often by an assembling covey. But if you do hunt Huns much, you will require a good lunch and a siesta. Walking is the name of the game when Hun hunting. In a sense it is monotonous walking too, for the stubble fields in which you will find the birds until mid-morning, and again in the late afternoon, are look-alike expanses of flat or gently rolling land. During the middle of the day the dried-out potholes, their brush fringes providing the only visual relief from monotony, will provide shelter for resting birds.

For this kind of hunting you should have a big-going brace of dogs. They'll save you a lot of steps. Because it's flat and open country, a dog can run as big as he will and still be seen. Then as you head in a general route cross-country putting miles on your boot soles, you need make side-excursions only to a dog on point instead of walking out every likely looking area. You could never adequately cover a large stubble-field without a dog, for the birds would run and elude you, never leaving the field and never taking wing.

In more limited country, however, it is possible to walk up Huns without a dog, or even better, to use a well-trained spaniel or retriever who will walk at heel to flush birds you cannot stir up and to pick up the shot birds. (Because of the sparsely grown terrain they inhabit, downed Huns are easier to recover than virtually any other game bird, despite their ability to blend into "bare" ground when alive. Even so, a good reliable retriever is always insurance.)

A few years back, I learned to hunt Huns this way in Sheboygan and Manitowoc counties in eastern Wisconsin. My mentor was Glen Popple, a veteran Sheboygan County game warden and one of the better wing shots I have enjoyed shooting with.

The first covey flushed near a drainage-ditch bank at least a hundred and fifty yards away from us. I turned to Glen in dismay. He grinned. "Mark where they come down," he advised. They settled in about eighty acres away. When we reached the area from which the birds had lifted, I couldn't keep the two Labradors at heel any longer; as they bustled about the scent-filled area, the older of the dogs swirl-tailed down a slight furrow, and a single straggler from the covey went out. Glen killed it. Clinker fetched it.

We were still a hundred yards from the ragweed stand where I'd marked the birds down when they got out a second time. "What the hell!" I exclaimed. "Aren't we ever going to get into that covey?"

"Patience, friend, patience." Glen consoled me. "We got closer this time, didn't we?"

We walked them up again, this time from seventy yards out, and

I had all I could do to keep from trying a futile shot. But the secret of Hungarian hunting without a dog or with a flushing dog at heel is to keep walking them up without shooting until you get close enough to shoot and shoot well.

Each time we jumped this covey they were a little closer. We picked off a couple of stragglers after a couple of rises. Finally, on the *sixth* rise, after about two miles of walking, the birds held until we got up to twenty yards from them. By then we were really in the mood to chew them up, and we did.

"That's enough out of that covey," Glen said. "Let's get back to the car and go work on another."

Maybe all this work isn't worth it. I know it isn't to a lot of hunters. But it just happens that I like to walk and I like to hunt Huns. I only wish I got more chance to do it.

Although it's a covey bird, you will generally find fewer Hun coveys in any given area than you will quail. The number of birds in a covey will also usually be less, at least in relatively settled regions. As far as birds are concerned, northern climes and conditions are not as salubrious as those prevailing in the quail country, which may account for this disparity. During the winter, with snow blanketing what meager cover there is in the flat farmlands the Hun likes, this species is a "sittin' duck" for winged predators.

On the Canadian prairies permission to hunt the vast lands once the crop has been harvested is usually an accepted thing or, if not, it is easily obtained. Farmers in the States are not quite so generous, but if you've located some Huns and are polite about it you can probably enter posted lands.

It may also pay you to ask questions of game wardens, rural mail carriers, landowners and others who are in the rural areas daily; they can save you much hunting around if they are willing to tell where they're spotted coveys. Huns usually attract attention because they congregate in groups and have an unusual appearance in comparison with more common birds.

If you're scouting on your own, look for flat country. Hilly or broken land, heavily wooded areas, wilderness tracts and brush don't attract and hold birds. But where there is agriculture—stubble fields, corn, weed-grown former pastures, sparsely grassed open fields with narrow fence-row or brush borders, these will hold Huns. When the snow gets deep in the winter drive the rural roads and use binoculars to spot coveys on stubble or manured fields. Figure on hunting that area next fall. The Huns should be there.

HUN GUNS AND LOADS

What gun and what load for Hungarian partridge? How about you telling me? I wish I could be specific and say "shoot such and such size shot out of such and such a barrel." But I can't

When it comes to the right load and the proper choke, if there ever was a game bird for gamblers it's the Hungarian partridge. Go out with a bird dog and figure to get some close-up shooting and what happens? The devious little dastards run out from under the dog and flush wild, and you don't have enough pattern or enough pellet-energy with your quail and woodcock gun and load to get out there and really smack 'em.

Next time though, you're gonna fool 'em! You come loaded for bear—or wild-flushing Huns. You've got your pheasant or duck gun, tightly choked and primed with max loads of No. 5 or 6 shot. But do you know what's gonna happen when you step into the field with that armament? They're going to sit tight to the dog, or let you walk up close after only a couple of flushes. And you'll only manage one bird out of the covey because you had to wait until they were out a bit, either out of fear of missing with the tight pattern or because whoever is doing the cooking detests hamburgered Hungarians.

You've probably figured it out for yourself by now, but the best solution is something I usually counsel against in shooting. Compromise!

The situation is this. The Hun is a relatively small bird which, if properly handled by a pointing dog, should be getting up close. This calls for something like No. 8 shot out of an open barrel, and a quick-handling gun so you'll get off more than just a single shot on the covey rise. This would be great if everything worked out right. But these little rascals are as fickle as the Gabor sisters are supposed to be. They just don't cooperate. They may jump up way out.

Furthermore, in contrast to other light boned, light feathered birds they're tough—tough enough to absorb a pretty good dose of fine shot at some distance and keep right on going. At the same time, they'll hold just enough for quail-type shots so that a man doesn't want to over-load or over-choke either.

A gambler who likes to hedge when he can will use a modified choke with No. 7½, high-base loads. Also heartily recommended is the 12 gauge. Those "pigeon loads," three and a quarter drams equivalent, and one and a quarter ounces of 7 or 7½ shot are also fine. If you're afraid you're going to have to get "reachy," the full-choke can be even better, and you might seriously consider No. 6 shot with either boring.

But it's been said before and here goes again: An awful lot of the concern about proper shot size and loads will take care of itself if the man pointing his favorite cannon swings properly.

For example, once on a hunting jaunt to Saskatchewan, my prime target had been waterfowl. But we'd wound up doing a good deal of sharptail and Hun hunting and the supply of upland loads for my 20-gauge got a bit critical. About all I had left in 20 gauge were some No. 4 "baby mags" loaded with one and one-eighth ounces of shot, with which I'd been killing ducks.

Now I have no idea how this would print on a pattern board—but the Huns were holding pretty good to the dogs and I sure didn't want "miss or massacre" shooting out of the full-choke barrel, so I put on the skeet barrel. I figured that even with No. 4 shot the added eighth of an ounce would give me an adequately dense, well-dispersed pattern. Apparently it did; at least I *claimed* my share on every covey rise, even though I lacked full confidence in the load.

Wouldn't a variable-choke compensating device be just the ticket for tricky Huns? Perhaps for you, but not for me. Just as I might pay too much attention to the choice of load that's shoved in the magazine, I'd be constantly concerned over whether I had the right tube, or the cone properly adjusted, when I should be concentrating on clipping a bird.

So when it comes to guns and loads for Huns I have no dogmatic advice to dish out. You gamble with your bright ideas and I'll keep right on, "win some, lose some," with mine. I just hope we both get a little luck.

HUN SHOOTING

As with sharp-tailed grouse and prairie chicken, the type of shooting required to knock down Hungarian partridge can best be learned and polished on a more frequently encountered bird, the bobwhite quail.

You'll face many of the same problems that we've discussed in regard to bobwhite shooting, chief among which is the disconcerting covey rise. The rules of thumb are also the same—concentrate on one bird at a time, get on them fast, and keep your eyes up and to the front when going in to flush.

However, the Hun is not a bobwhite. These gray partridge are not as gentlemanly in their behavior before a dog, and you may find them flushing some distance out in front, for, like the pheasant, they are not reluctant to trust their legs instead of their wings.

Even though they eschew any type of cover and are wide-open targets, the Huns make up for this by getting away with more speed than quail, and once their whirring wing beats reach top speed they are really fast flyers. This combination makes a double on a covey rise a much more satisfying accomplishment than on quail. Seldom will a shotgunner seriously consider taking a third shot on Huns.

While they like to run and flush wild, once these birds decide to sit tight they will sit very tight. You may find yourself walking through them in cover you didn't think could conceal a grasshopper, only to have them explode all around you or go out behind you. Huns also like to scatter in all directions. This can shake you up enough to cause a lot of shot to go awry rather than putting birds on the stubble.

As explained earlier, when walking up Huns they will get out at extreme ranges. This then becomes comparable to gunning prairie grouse and requires the same technique, with the added complication of having a smaller, faster target to work on.

So if Hun hunting is in your horoscope, and you will be hunting with pointing dogs, get your practice on quail. (If you're going to walk the birds up or use a flushing dog, there is really no other bird on which you can polish your shooting technique, for while pheasants or prairie grouse may flush just as wild, they are larger and slower.)

If you think you can score on snap shots at extreme range, approach your first Hun hunt with confidence. But if you are a "normal" shooter, just figure that this bird's perversity will keep you off-balance, and make you miss more shots than usual and you won't be disappointed.

6

Sharpies and Yellowlegs
THE PRAIRIE GROUSE

UNFORTUNATELY, when today's hunter speaks of gunning sharp-tailed grouse and prairie chicken, particularly the latter, he is usually talking nostalgically about the past, rather than optimistically about the future.

For the bulk of United States hunters, good hunting—or even *any* hunting—for these two oft-confused species of upland game birds is non-existent. They have gone the way of the windmill on the farm and steam locomotive train service to small towns.

There are, however, still remnant, huntable populations of these birds in areas of a few Northern and Plains states and on the Canadian prairies. Any man who gets a chance to go after these grand birds should snap it up. Because that chance still exists, and out of respect for one of the most interesting birds I've ever hunted, they are included in this book.

I have lumped these two separate species together as "prairie grouse," both in the interest of space and because it makes sense. This dawned on me the first time I hunted these birds in Nebraska. There and then both birds were listed as prairie grouse and the bag limit (just two per day, as they are trophy birds) included either sharptailed grouse or prairie chicken.

Where the ranges of these two birds overlap, they look so much alike and are so unfamiliar to most hunters that honest mistakes are easily made under the stress of getting on a wild-flushing bird in a hurry. When different rules apply to each of the two species some inadvertent violators get hurt, and the "wrong" birds are often wasted.

My home state does this sort of thing in still permitting a short open season on sharp-tailed grouse, though it has not had an open season on prairie chicken for almost a decade. Surely not one hunter in a hundred can spot the difference between the two birds in flight and many can't do it even with the dead bird in hand.

(However, before criticizing too freely, I should acknowledge that Wisconsin is striving valiantly to preserve a remnant flock of native prairie chicken in the one management area of the state in which they still exist. The hunter or two who takes time to find and hunt the few sharptails which remain elsewhere in the state is probably interested enough to know the difference, and in any case, the odd chicken illegally shot couldn't restore a huntable population. So there are arguments both ways.)

In any case, these birds have always been confused by many people. Practically all the natives in areas where there are sharptailed grouse refer to them as "chickens." So do bird-dog trainers and field trialers. Today, when someone tells you he's going "chicken hunting" it's a safe bet he's after sharptails.

To make clear the difference between prairie chicken and sharptailed grouse, the ornithologists prefer calling the prairie chicken a "pinnated grouse," that name stemming from the twin tufts of stiff feathers based on each side of the neck that can be raised above the head so they look like horns. These are called *pinnae*. The chicken's Latin label is *Tympanuchus cupido americanus*.

The sharp-tailed grouse is just slightly larger than the prairie chicken and is saddled with the Latin name of *Pediocetes phasianellus*. While sometimes enjoying the same wide-open spaces the prairie chicken needs to exist, the sharptail can also adapt to the more northern climes and gets by in country where there is more brush and less grass than is ideal for prairie chicken habitat.

So you want to know how to tell the difference? In flight it is extra-difficult if you are shooting, since you must get on these birds fast and they are often a long way out.

But look for the feature which gives the sharptail its name. You'll find that the tail of a prairie chicken is square, rather than pintailed. This along with the color impression the bird gives, and a knowledge of which species *should* be in the area, will aid your identification. (To me, the sharptail always shows more silvery in color than the prairie chicken.)

Once you have the bird in your hand, identification is easy, though in glancing through my "bird books" I couldn't find one ornithologist who gives the quickest way I know to differentiate between the two species. They spend a lot of ink trying to describe color. The breast of the sharptail, you are also told, has V markings while the breast of the prairie chicken is barred. (Usually I can't remember which and besides, I'm a leg man myself.) So at the risk of giving you spurious information (since the experts ignore it) my advice is to examine the legs.

If the bird in your hand has yellow legs, it's a prairie chicken. If the legs are gray, even going black, the bird is a sharp-tailed grouse. As a matter of fact, in my youth I seldom heard hunters refer to the birds by their proper name. The chicken was always "Ol' yellowlegs" and the sharptail was referred to as "Gray leg" or "Black foot."

In the heat of a hunt the sharptail can be confused with a ruffed grouse or a hen pheasant. (Occasionally this happens when a bird or two of the other species strays into sharptail country and gets up in thick cover. Prairie grouse are heavier-bodied birds, therefore a bit larger than ruffed grouse.)

More than any of our other upland birds, woodcock excepted, the prairie grouse tend to be migratory. They "pack up" in the fall, particularly in the far northern range, and whether they move south or stick around locally they can make an exciting spectacle with their large numbers. Unfortunately, however, the numbers have dwindled until few persons now see what was once a common sight and an attraction for the market hunter.

I've resided on land in what was once "chicken" country. My first father-in-law often referred to "the clouds of prairie chicken" that used to lift from the marsh-bordered fields in the fall. This was into the 1930s. Before that city hunters used to drive out to hunt chickens in horse and buggy. In the really good prairie grouse country to the west, special trains used to bring in wealthy hunters from the large cities to the south. I've talked with men who lived in plush railroad cars parked on sidings so they could hunt chickens in the grand manner into the 1920s.

Up until after World War II, hunters used to come to a marsh across the road I could gaze on while I was waiting to hunt ol' yellowlegs. Now it serves as a public waterfowl hunting area managed by the department of natural resources.

I shot my last chicken in Wisconsin in the late 1950s, the last year the season was open. There were still a few birds left to hunt in west-central Wisconsin and a close friend of mine, Vince Skilling, a conservation law enforcement supervisor from Oshkosh, had been a game warden in that area and he knew where to find the birds. My last sharptails were taken a few years later in northwestern Wisconsin. Since then I have hunted both species in Nebraska and now I go to Canada for sharptail hunting.

This has been the story of the prairie grouse and the prairie grouse hunter over the past seventy years. Yet in the days of yore the birds were plentiful enough to darken the skies, and the Great Lakes and the Great Plains states were happy hunting grounds for market hunters with strings of dogs scouring the country ahead of them so horse-drawn buckboards could be loaded with birds to ship to the Eastern market.

Even the unrestricted market hunting didn't sound the death knell on these birds. After World War I the demand for wheat saw grazing lands in the West broken up and planted. When drought and depression hit the nation in the 1930s, winds eroded the topsoil that was once held by grass. The result was a dustbowl where nothing lived.

While on the Western plains the exploiters "did in" the prairie grouse, in heavily timbered states like Wisconsin, lumbermen and forest fires actually made a home for them. When clear cutting ended and the "big burns" were prevented or quickly suppressed, the large openings known as "cut-over" began to be filled by normal plant succession. Later on they were systematically planted with conifers.

But the clearings made by the lumberjack and scoured out by fires approximated small prairies, covered with grass, dotted with snags and stumps and interspersed with brush. This was a home for the sharptail and chicken. The years following World War I were also great ones for "reclaiming lands" and drainage projects by the dozens turned marshes into grassland and cropland. For a time the prairie grouse benefited. But when these projects were abandoned they either reverted to marsh or became too overgrown to furnish a home for the birds of the open prairie.

Even agriculture, as it was practiced up until World War II, often made it possible for at least small flocks of prairie grouse to "make out," for a family could still be raised on forty acres. The cut-over and marsh country was dotted with "stump farms" which were little if any advanced from the pioneer farms of seventy-five to a hundred years before. Grain was shocked and marsh hay was mowed, but no one ever quite caught up on the land he wanted to clear and livestock grazed in "wild pastures."

All this is gone now. It may soon be gone in the western provinces of Canada where sharptail habitat is broken up yearly to grow more wheat. In many areas the sharptail is now largely replaced by the stubble-field-loving Hungarian partridge.

In the matter of prairie grouse, man both proposeth and disposeth. In Wisconsin every effort is being expended to maintain the prairie chicken in at least a show-place setting on the Buena Vista marsh in Adams and Portage counties. But ironically this is not a "natural" chicken habitat that once held birds with no conscious aid from man. It was originally a waterfowl area, despoiled by a huge drainage project and later abandoned to grass. Commercial bluegrass growers then cultivated it and birds thrived. But the market dropped out of that and it was once again abandoned. For almost forty years now it has been artificially managed in an effort to maintain conditions as they were when economics dictated they be so.

Wildlife experts may know what to do to restore some semblance of prairie-grouse hunting. But most must admit, at least privately, that as long as economic factors dictate our way of life, there is little that can be done. Their requirements being what they are, prairie grouse are extremely difficult to "manage." Therefore, even when suitable habitat is available, the ambitious and practical game manager and administrator seems bent on converting it or adapting it to support some more manageable species, virtually assured of short-sighted public support.

That's why most hunters whose memory stretches back almost a half-century speak of chicken hunting with nostalgia. The general loss of this wonderful native bird is a black mark on the face of the nation. But hunting should be a happy thing. So let's move on to something more enjoyable, the infrequent hunts furnished by the remnant flocks of prairie grouse.

PRAIRIE-GROUSE TACTICS, GUNS AND LOADS

Even as the lithe white and black pointer flowed across the tufted grasslands, purposefully reaching for the "bluff" a full quarter-mile away, a man's thoughts could not help but stray from hunting.

"The wide open spaces" may have become a trite phrase. But this is wonderful country to be in, whether you're talking about the rough prairies of Saskatchewan or the rolling Sandhills country of Nebraska. For in any area where nothing obstructs the vision until the land and the sky merge, it is not hard to imagine why the plainsman and the cowboy reveled in their lonely existence, or why the Indian fought so strenuously for the impressive grasslands that were once termed "the great American desert."

Suddenly the excited flagging of the dog's tail brings you back to reality and the present; for this is where the prairie grouse are, and now the dreamer becomes a hunter.

The momentary cessation of movement by the dog, and then its careful, studied stalk, with each foot going down softly, precisely and deliberately, alerts you to the fact that what the dog has located are not "virgin" birds. You feared this when you saw the tire tracks criss-crossing the grazing lands, for they indicated that these birds had been hunted and hunted hard. (The "do-it-the-easy-way" boys work the bird country with jeeps and pick-up trucks, since "chickens" are thinly spread over these multiple acres: they will put up to a mile between them and a hunter when flushed, and once shot over, they are wary and willing to run and flush wild.)

Fortunately, your birds are reluctant to leave the heavy cover provided by the brush and stunted aspen that make up what Canadians call "bluffs" (strips of cover, usually bordering swales dotting the grazing lands). On the previous day the intelligent pointer bitch learned her business and adapted to this "new" bird; she freezes.

You and your hunting partner proceed briskly but without un-due haste considering the circumstances. The slower, closer working German Wirehaired Pointer precedes you, and for a moment you are afraid he may not see the bitch on point, will come in wrong on the wind and "bump" the birds. So you shout a cautioning "Whoaup!" just as the old dog spots his motionless bracemate. There is no prettier tableau. Clear blue sky, gray-green prairie grass, frost-seared foliage, a point and a back.

The first bird gets out when you are still five yards behind and to the right of the pointing dog. It's on your side of the cover and as you swing you hear the "cuck, cuck" cackle of another bird going out on your partner's side. It disconcerts you. Slow in getting under way and big bodied, the sharptail looks almost awkward as he breaks across the swale. You miss, but your partner doesn't.

As you lower your gun, a third bird gets out. This is a tougher shot, halfway between a straightaway and a right angle, but you get it. You remain alert as the dogs seek the downed birds, but by the time the retrieves are made, you are sure that the small covey numbered only three.

This is sharptail hunting at its best. There's no mass eruption, like a flock of Huns or a covey of quail. The birds like to get out singly and in pairs. This is distracting in itself for there is often a bird rising just as you come up on the one in the air.

Your skeet-barreled, 20-gauge pump throwing No. 5 shot and the 6's pushed out of your partner's 12-gauge autoloader were adequate at these ranges. But there have been and there will be other times and other places when other tactics and other equipment will be called for.

You may watch a flock of a dozen birds pitch in on a high knoll half a mile distant. You walk to them, close enough to see some heads protruding from the sparse grass cover. But before you can get close enough for even an optimist to shoot, the old sentinel bird sets off the alarm and the flock leaves to plane down even a greater distance away . . . .

You've walked for hours. You've seen plenty of good sign—rose hips, that pretty red prairie bud that always means chickens, depressions in the grass filled with neat piles of white-tipped dung where birds have roosted—but you've seen no birds.

The cover has gotten really rough and you've pulled half a dozen little cactus buds off your limping dogs. But they still go on. They both disappear. Then not seventy-five yards to your right front your pointer comes over the rise and in mid-stride, slams down motionless. "Point! She's got 'em," you shout to your partner. As you wait for him to hurry to you across the hundred yards of short ground cover that separates you, you ease up toward the dog, looking in the direction she's pointing.

That's when you discover it was not her find at all. Like the lady she is, she is backing—honoring the find of the German Wirehair who is standing with docked tail erect, eyes focused right in front of him. Thicker coated, thicker skinned, slower and more deliberate, he penetrated the thicket and found a tight-sitting bird the faster dog had missed as she skimmed the edges.

The flushed bird proves an easy shot. For some, this reward would not be adequate for an hour and a half of walking. But it's all a chicken hunter can ask—and all the shots are not that easy! Remember the bird your partner walked up that came rocketing over your left front? You could easily have excused yourself for missing. But you folded the bird and he hit the parched bare ground so hard his feathers flew.

You remember a good shot all your life. It's something to savor, like the first gulp of near-scalding coffee from the morning's cook fire, the first bite of whatever is available when you haven't eaten all day, or a woman who tells you how much she appreciates your being a man and knows how to prove it.

Then there was the long shot on the second of two birds flushed off a knoll as he pitched down the steep slope toward the arroyo bottom. It was a strong sixty yards and perhaps you had no business touching off, even with a full-choked 12-gauge and No. 4 shot. But you did, and the bird skidded into the grass. The little white and liver Springer Spaniel bitch beat the big black Labrador to the bird. They had been put down to work the thick stuff the sharpies were loafing in during midday. Her eyes were all smiles as she delivered.

Yet that shot had followed a frustrating early morning when the birds were out in the frosted grasslands, and would not sit for the pointers in that sparse cover. The way they sneaked out and flushed could fracture the heart of man and dog. (Early-season coveys, which are actually immature broods of the year, hold for dogs in the classic manner, and that's when to work them with a young dog. Later in the season it takes a seasoned performer, preferably one who has proven he can solve the problem of running pheasants.)

You may well hunt chickens and sharptails under conditions that drive you to picking up your dogs. I once drove two thousand miles in two days just to hunt with Bob Munger, a writing buddy from Nebraska who wanted to show me the Sandhills country. I never regretted it, although the birds sure were hard to come by.

Heat better than 85 degrees and a pernicious crop of sandburrs soon decommissioned my old German Wirehair, Briar. He was worthless that hunt—the only time he produced a bird was when he sought the shade of a shelter belt, and practically laid down on a pair.

But this tipped us off. We hiked back to the car and let out the Springer spaniel and the Labrador retriever I'd brought along in case we decided to try for ducks in the prairie potholes or along the Loup River. They rooted out birds siesta-ing in the cottonwood stands, the shelter belts and other skimpy cover that provided relief from the sun and dry wind, and we had some great shooting.

On another day, when hunting with a local rancher, and using the Springer as a retriever, we had long shooting. We needed all the choke and all the shot they can build in gun and shells. Bob broke the wing of a downhill-gliding chicken on one of those impossibly far-out shots that keep a man's hunting fever up. Then it gave Flirt, the Springer, a merry chase among the rolled hay bales that dotted the rangeland.

The last bird of the day, late in the afternoon, flushed wild and dropped in on a knoll. We marked it, hiked to it, climbed the knoll and stood near the crest, baffled at not producing a bird, when ol' yellow-legs decided to whirr out. (Chickens like to sit on promontories—don't pass them up.)

I hurried my shot because Bob and I have a needling contest when we hunt together, and there are no holds barred in beating the other to a shot. It was a low straightaway and the bird fell.

Our timing and reflexes are so often identical that I played safe before claiming the bird and turned to Bob. "Did you shoot?" He grinned as he lowered his autoloader. "Nope," he shook his head. "But you just better believe there wasn't any slack left in the trigger."

Maybe you'd have preferred that I tell you how to hunt prairie grouse in textbook, rather than anecdotal fashion. But that would be unfair to chicken hunting, which is a sport a man should enjoy, one hunt at a time, and then take pleasure in recounting for the unfortunates who have never tasted this delicacy.

But I have tried, in the course of tale spinning, to advise you what kind of country to seek, the conditions you'll encounter, the tactics to employ, and the dogs, guns and loads that will add to your score. I'd appreciate if you'd hunt a little for the information, just as you would hunt for birds in the wild.

In conclusion, never conclude a prairie-grouse hunt without a touch of sadness. For among all the upland bird species we've hunted together in this book, the prairie grouse are the prime condidates for obliteration from the hunting scene. For they cannot be said to be holding their own. And while it is fine to preserve a few birds for posterity, as far as the hunter is concerned once the shooting of a species is banned, it might as well be extinct.

So never forget to make a special effort to recall how everything happened, how it looked, how it sounded, how it smelled and *how it felt*. For every prairie-grouse hunt might well be your last.

PRAIRIE-GROUSE SHOOTING

This section can be brief, for there are only two "styles" that are successful in gunning prairie chicken and sharp-tailed grouse, and both have been discussed at length in earlier chapters.

If flushed from a "bluff," a shelter belt or some other cover edge where they've sought shade in midday, or refuge to rest up, the chicken or sharpie may get out when you are on the wrong side of the cover or may manage to put something between you.

But for the most part, the birds inhabit essentially rangeland or other such grassy habitat, and the shooting is open. Early in the season, when the coveys haven't been shot up and the young birds of the year haven't wised up, you'll be able to kill prairie grouse on the rise if you've mastered bobwhite shooting. That is, provided the birds are out on the prairie.

If your dog should pin a covey on the brush edge, the shooting may more closely approach ruffed-grouse gunning, though you will be out in the clear, and the prairie grouse show little inclination to dodge and side-slip through cover the way Ol' Ruff does. In both instances the prairie grouse is both a larger and slower target.

Later in the season, when the birds are wary and running out from under even the best of pointing dogs, or anytime, if you are foolish enough to try walking them up without a dog, you'd better practice up on your long-range shooting.

Successfully knocking down spooky "chickens" is a shotgun art all in itself. In this shooting situation the finely honed, reflexive skills of the crack Northeastern ruffed grouse and woodcock shot or the Southern quail shooter won't be much help.

Probably the nearest thing to compare with it in wild bird shooting is gunning for wild-flushing pheasants. But if there is any practice that will do a hunter some good the first time he tries to gun prairie grouse, it's probably shooting trap from handicap yardage.

What makes the "chicken" so sporting is that although it's in the open, it gets out at such a distance from the hunter that he must get on that bird with no waste time or motion. At the same time, while he has to get on quick, he cannot "poke and hope" as he does on close-rising birds.

When a hunter spots a bird rising forty to fifty yards out in front of him, he must not only act quickly but must also point his gun precisely and swing smoothly. It's some of the most challenging shooting on the North American continent. Fortunately, prairie grouse do not soak up shot the way pheasants do—just a few pellets will discourage them and they'll hit the ground.

Though the possibility is remote, I suppose I should at least mention what happens if you encounter a flight of birds coming to a grainfield to feed in the evening—you "drive" this field as you would in a pheasant drive, and the shooting is similar.

This is almost too easy a way to hunt these birds, but it's probably academic, anyway. There's little chance that you'll get this type of shooting either today or in the future, for wild "chicken" shooting now seems restricted to the devoted few who will treat this once-common game bird as a trophy.

7

Learning To Hit
Upland Game

BACK in those not too distant days when some millions of Uncle Sammy's soldiers returned to civilian life after World War II, quite a few of them trundled off to college.

For the would-be hunter who wanted to make the most of it this was a golden opportunity. For a couple of years, I managed to schedule my classes so I could make it out to Lake Poygan for the early morning duck flights and still get back to make my 9 or 10 o'clock's. (There were also times when a particularly inviting looking piece of pheasant cover on the way back just couldn't be overlooked, and the wisdom dished out by a various assortment of professors on such days was not mine to have and to hold.)

This is no way to graduate *summa cum laude*, I found. College administrators are inclined to frown not only on unexplained absences, but on the presence of hunting dogs and the captive pigeons and mallard ducks so vital to the education of a gun dog. But fortunately for me, Lawrence College officials developed a special tolerance toward ex-servicemen in those days.

Furthermore, game was more plentiful and accessible, and while the "Hindenburg Line" and the "Big Cane" were filled with waterfowl gunners at opening time every day, hunter numbers hadn't yet peaked. Even more important to me was the accessibility to upland game on private lands that were not yet posted against trespass.

The economics of a poor college student going hunting virtually every day of the season were something else. But a government subsistence allowance for attending school partly took care of that, and the foresight of having gotten married my freshman year did the rest. My wife worked.

Lest you get the impression that to be a successful hunter you must be a lazy good-for-nothing, just let me say that, besides working summers on construction crews, during the "off-season" part of the school term I managed to put in sixty hours a week on a "part-time" job on a newspaper in addition to carrying full-credit courses in college. But as you have guessed, I majored in hunting when the bird seasons were open and have continued to make this my chief vocation in the fall months.

All this may not seem germane to the subject of passing out information on how to learn to clobber game birds in flight, but the purpose of this little discourse is to set the stage so a profound truth about shooting can be illustrated. For it was during this period that I discovered that no one can become even a passable shot on any type of game bird if he doesn't shoot a gun both frequently and without concern for the "sure thing" or the cost of ammunition.

There were other hookey-playing hunters enrolled in school, Tom being one of them. Tom had done some duck hunting and was a fair-to-middlin' shot. But he had never hunted any upland game except for a few pheasant. He wanted to.

The fact that my wife's father owned a 160-acre farm that contained and bordered on some excellent partridge-hunting land had absolutely nothing to do with my marrying her. It was a fortunate coincidence. So Tom, my old English Cocker, a young Labrador retriever and I sneaked off one morning and headed my jalopy for my father-in-law's farm.

The birds were "up." In a matter of two and a half hours along the bank of the Embarrass River the dogs flushed twenty-one ruffed grouse. When we got back to the car for a sandwich the score was as follows:

I had fired thirteen shots with my compensator-equipped Sears-Roebuck 12-gauge. I had four partridge in my game bag. Tom had not once fired his Model-12 Winchester.

The birds and the cover had baffled him completely. I have seen this happen since, but on a more limited scale. He had many shooting opportunities—*partridge* shooting opportunities. But he was geared to shooting waterfowl, taking open shots which give a man time to lead his birds deliberately. Sometimes in the thick cover Tom never even bothered to raise the gun. "I was waiting for an open shot," he said. Other times, when the bird broke across an opening, it was gone before he completed his deliberate swing. On a few occasions, early in the hunt, I held off shooting to give Tom first crack at a flushed bird, only to watch it wing off without even a futile salvo to hasten it along.

Perhaps Tom later learned to shoot upland game. I don't know, for we never again hunted together. Could be he thought I was hogging the shooting. In any case, I felt sorry for him, and nobody likes to hunt with a shooter he feels sorry for. It's much more fun to hunt with a good shot—then you can needle and kid about the misses, knowing you aren't treading on a painful truth.

Anyhow, the experience illustrated two things to me. First, the obvious truth that good intentions and desire aren't going to make flying birds fall dead. You have to take your shots under the conditions the bird and cover impose upon you and to hell with the distinct possibility that you might miss. Secondly, being a passable shot on one kind of game bird does not guarantee that you'll be able to shoot for sour apples on a different species, particularly on your first few hunts.

Perhaps some of the personal experiences I've used in trying to explain how to shoot various kinds of game birds under various situations sound like bragging. But if the tales of my hits overshadow those detailing my misses it is for illustrative purposes *to assist you*, not to bolster my ego. I have also learned from missing —all too frequently. No doubt you will too.

No one is ever going to mistake me for Annie Oakley—I mean, even in the masculine version. But at least I have reached a point where I am mildly surprised when I swing, pull and the bird doesn't come down. I mind the time when I was greatly surprised and wildly elated when I shot and something fell. If you are absolutely stunned and unbelieving if the bird doesn't fold every time you touch off, *you* can tell *me* how to shoot.

There are very few persons hunting today who don't have quite a bit to learn about shooting. The unfortunate thing is that adult American males suffer from some kind of a psychosis when it comes to taking shooting instructions. Helping out at gun clinics and various private tutorings, I've found that women and children soak up good shooting instruction as cheap raincoats absorb water. But men? Unh, Unh! Put shotguns in the hands of ten neophyte adult male shooters and nine of them will tell the instructor how it ought to be done.

The time they should spend listening and doing, they will waste regaling the hapless gentleman who's volunteered to help them with accounts of the hunting trips they've been on and lies about the difficult shots they consistently score in the field.

Responsibility for this attitude may stem from the myth that all male Americans are born with guns in their hands and just naturally know how to use them properly. Therefore, with no loss of pride or manhood, red blooded he-men will submit to the teachings of a golf pro, or turn their sons over to a football or basketball coach for training in those sports. But you insult a man and call him a sissy if you imply there's something about shooting he doesn't know, or that he isn't prepared to teach his son everything he needs to know about shooting.

They say it takes a thief to know one. So I know this to be a truth, not only because I've run into it in attempting to show others how to shoot but because I went through that stage myself. I happened to be fortunate in running into a man whom I respected enough to listen to and who managed to make me see the light.

My own father died before I was four. So having no misguided adult instruction to complicate matters, the blame for my poor shooting rested solely on my own shoulders. What I learned about shooting I picked up by trial and error. I kept telling myself I was a "better-than-average" shot until I was almost convinced. If you didn't realize that my dogs provided me with more than my share of shooting chances, the birds in my bag might even have convinced you. But the fact is that I was a miserable shot.

I was in my mid-twenties and "working" full-time as an outdoor writer on a metropolitan newspaper when I bumped into Bill Johnson, an exhibition shooter for Remington-Peters. Whether he believed half the stuff I was handing out about being able to shoot or really intended to show me the error of my ways, Bill never said. But in any event when I showed up to cover a Wisconsin State Skeet Shoot for the paper, he informed me he had entered me in the event.

GAME WARDENS

You don't talk game wardens out of anything. But, despite all the lies they've heard, conservation law enforcement agents can be compassionate in the excercise of good judgement.

Be truthful if a warden questions you and, after an encounter with an understanding "brush cop" who "goes easy on you", don't brag about how you outsmarted him. Likely you didn't. A warden likes to make "good pinches" but takes no pride or enjoyment from arrests on technicalities. He may choose to believe you are an honest sportsman who has made an inadvertant mistake. Live up to his trust. If you do get slapped with a "ticket" take it like a man and remember wardens don't make the laws. They enforce them. If they make a human mistake, your day in court should rectify it.

Without those men patrolling game coverts at all hours our hunting would be in a sorry state. If game laws are not enforced, even the sportsman who wants to do right will become disgusted at game thievery with impunity and cheat in order to "get his share". Soon there's nothing left to share.

Do your best to understand the rules and regulations, complicated as they may be, and then bend over backwards to do right. Don't be afraid to contact a warden and ask questions. You'll find he'd rather steer you clear of trouble than issue a summons after you've gotten into difficulty.

If my prejudices and sympathies show, blame it on the two hunting seasons I spent working as a conservation warden. It was an educational experience every sportsman ought to share.

For me it was a degrading debacle. While women and little children were grinding up clay birds with monotonous regularity I went out and scratched down a sum total of 55 X 100. I tried to sneak away, but Bill collared me. A practical psychologist as well as a top flight shooter, he said, "At least you had guts enough to go out there and try it. That's more than I can say for most of you typewriter experts. Now do you want to learn how to shoot?"

I did. We spent a number of afternoons on the trap and skeet ranges. Not too many. But after the fundamentals were explained I shot at every opportunity. We achieved no miracles, but the following year I did finish runner-up in the Class D all-bore event at the State Shoot with a 94 X 100. (A twelve-year-old lad beat me out in the shoot-off to keep everything in its proper perspective, or I might not have learned anything beyond that.)

So what I'm going to suggest is that if you're really serious about learning to clobber game birds on the wing, you ought to make haste to find yourself a qualified marksman who can actually *show* you a few things. Ask for advice, listen to him and do what he tells you. You may be able to make changes or adaptations later. But at least you'll have a proper start.

The best place to find such a man, if you don't number an accomplished shooter among your acquaintances, is a gun club in your locality. Keep an eye on the newspapers for announcements about gun clinics and shooting lessons. Arms and ammunition companies conduct these affairs, and offer professional shooters as instructors. So do conservation clubs and some civic organizations.

Just pocket your pride and that worthless conceit and make an attempt to learn something. You'll never regret it.

Sure, I know that the practice you get in shooting those little old discs isn't anything like gunning wild birds. You don't have to tell me that. But don't try to tell me you're a dead-eye on the real thing if you can't hit half of the clay birds that are flung out there. I may not call you a liar, but I'll sure think it.

Shooting at clay targets on a trap or skeet field is not comparable to shooting wild game on the wing for the simple reason that seldom, if ever, do two live birds fly at the same angle and same speed under identical conditions. (And if they do, it's been too long between shots for you to remember just what you did and adjust to that speed and angle.) Clay-target shooting *can be* more or less mechanically taught because the speeds and angles are constant. That's why good trap and skeet shooting is a skill, while good wing shooting on game birds is an art.

But no artist is going to be good until he masters some of the mechanics of his craft. That's what clay-bird shooting will allow you to do. Unless you are unusually blessed, there are no longer enough natural flying targets left in this world of ours to allow you to master the fundamentals of wing shooting in much less than a lifetime. Those clay birds are flying targets. Shoot all of them that you can, on a regular trap or skeet field, or thrown with a hand trap out in a pasture or field.

Utilize this artificial means until you can powder those clays consistently. Shoot during the off-season to keep brushed up. Believe me, you'll find it will help your wing shooting. For practice will make better, if not perfect, the designs you have on *any* flying target.

I hope you got the idea from the earlier story about my pheasant and duck shooting companions who never did get onto a partridge. But it's so important that I want to reinforce it with another tale— and you may or may not want to follow my example when introducing your own son to upland shooting.

Mike, when he turned twelve years of age (earliest legal hunting age in my home state), was big, strong and fairly well coordinated. He'd had quite a bit of shotgun handling and shooting experience on hand-thrown clay birds and crows since the age of seven.

For Christmas he received a 12-gauge Remington Model-1100 autoloader and a case of trap loads (not that we were loaded with dough that year, but I had an extra bird dog that was well started and swapped him for the gun and shells).

I do *not* believe in giving a boy a crooked-stocked, spur-hammered, single-shot pea-shooter as his first upland gun. Hell, if I can't hit anything with a monstrosity like that, how can I expect a beginner to? Furthermore, if a lad has any love of the sport at all, he won't be able to get his hands on a multiple-shot, well-balanced weapon fast enough. A good gun is a gift he'll really prize, and can use for a lifetime.

Safety? Making the first shot count? Every salesman has to have *some* pitch for the article he's trying to move, and too many fathers have bought this bill of goods. Actually I rate a hammer gun as *un*safe, because once you cock it, if you do not fire it, you must let the hammer down to return it to a safe position. Let a cold, stiff thumb slip and the tightly sprung hammer falls on the firing pin and—boom!

As far teaching a lad to make that first shot count rather than depending on the back-up loads in the magazine—it doesn't take Albert Einstein to figure out that if you give him only one shell at a time, ergo, you have made a single-shot gun out of any pump, autoloader or double. (Yes, I know there are bolt-action and lever-action shotguns. But who needs one?)

So the following fall we took off on Mike's first foray into ruffed-grouse lairs. We got home late for supper, something my wife should have grown accustomed to but which always set her up for an argument. We had seven or eight birds, the usual mixture of grouse and woodcock.

"How many did you shoot, Mike?" she asked. "One, I guess," he answered, which put me in line for a reaming. "Can't even give your own son a chance at those birds, can you?" she let loose. "I remember the one time I went out with you. By the time I first saw those darn birds you'd already shot twice. You'll discourage him just like you discouraged me—and maybe that's a good thing. I don't know if I can stomach two bird hunters in the house at the same time."

As calmly as possible, under the circumstances, I shouted my side of the story at her. "If he's going to go hunting with the men, he'd better learn to shoot like them. I did wait a couple of times for him to shoot and he never did. I'm damned if I'm going to stand around and watch those rascals get away without at least hurrying 'em along."

To make a long story short, the next season on opening day the first bird got up. My gun was halfway mounted when the bird dropped and the reverberation from Mike's 12-gauge reminded me I had a hunting companion. He didn't hit everything he shot at that day, not by a long shot—but very often the sounds of our guns blended as one, and he wound up shooting three birds out from under me. What slight feelings of guilt I had about shooting too fast evaporated in a hurry and since then, Mike has sure wiped my eye often enough to keep them from coming back!

8

Guns For The Uplands

FEW hunters can afford a whole cabinet full of guns. And even fewer can afford the time or money to be fitted out by a custom gunmaker. If you are one of the fortunates, fine and dandy—get the best that money will buy, and enjoy it in good health.

But if kids, mortgage payments or any other monetary drains affect your budget so that you have to carefully plan the purchase of a shotgun, the practical thing to do is to settle for one gun and learn to shoot it well. (It will probably do better for you than a flock of fancy guns does for the man who spends more time displaying his gun cabinet than he does shooting.) But how many bird hunters are that practical?

Gun buying is a rather incurable affliction of most hunters. I'm as guilty as the next guy. A new model shows up on the market and I hanker after it. As it is, I have half a dozen good shotguns that were going to be "just what I need" for a certain kind of hunting, and they hardly ever leave the house, while the old standbys burn up all the ammo. In a way it's fortunate I seldom corner more than a couple hundred bucks cash at a time or I'd have even more guns that see very little use.

Whether your gun cabinet consists of one lonely fusil or a dozen, this much is certain: you ought to have a gun—or a barrel—that has the right choke for every game bird you hunt. Anything less than that will cost you birds in the field.

The most important specification of the shotgun you buy will not be its fit, its type or its cost. The thing that should concern you first is this thing referred to as "choke."

Simply put, "choke" is the constriction in diameter, or lack of it, in the muzzle of your shotgun, that will determine how quickly the shot spreads out into a pattern of maximum killing efficiency once it leaves the barrel. The three most commonly referred-to chokes are cylinder (open), modified (half-closed), and full (tight) chokes. You will also encounter improved cylinder (which approximates what is also known as skeet boring and throws a somewhat tighter pattern than cylinder), you may bump into the tighter "improved" modified and may even hear some guy talking about "super-full."

Now, a full-choked gun should put at least 70 per cent of the shot pellets fired from one cartridge into the confines of a thirty-inch circle at a distance of forty yards. Conservatively, the modified would put about 50 to 55 per cent in that thirty-inch circle at the same distance, but only about 25 to 30 per cent would be scored by the cylinder bore.

To visualize what's happening, compare the choke to a garden hose. The full choke is comparable to the concentrated stream that holds together and will wash out a fresh seeding at close range, the cylinder to the finer spray that covers a large area but does not concentrate as much of its force at one pont.

What it means to you as a shooter is that a gun bored full-choke will throw out an extremely concentrated pattern at most of the ranges you'll be shooting birds at, causing you either to miss or mashing up the birds you do hit. Cylinder bore will aid you in taking the close shots since there is greater shot dispersion quicker, but it will cost you birds taken out beyond twenty-five or thirty yards. (The best borings for various game birds are discussed in detail in connection with each species.)

Much of the trouble in choosing a shotgun comes from the natural tendency to equate proficiency with size, quantity or abundance. The argument runs that if a 28-inch barrel shoots pretty good, a 30-incher must be better and a 32-inch "Long Tom" will be a real reacher. Stuff this gun with souped-up "baby magnum" loads of four drams equivalent of powder and one and a half ounces of shot and, look out! And since one shell will kill a bird, a gun that holds half a dozen should let me knock hell out of a whole flock. So it goes, and up to a point it makes some sense.

For if you like to shoot such larger birds as duck and pheasant, as well as ruffed grouse and quail, quite possibly your pet weapon was chosen for long-range use. You know those mallard and ring-neck can be out there pretty far at times and a man ought to have a tightly choked, long shootin' gun if he's gonna reach them.

	APPROX. PELLETS IN 1 OZ.	2385	585	410	350	225	170	135	90	50
SHOT	DIAM. IN INCHES	.05	.08	.09	.09½	.11	.12	.13	.15	.18
	NUMBER	• 12	• 9	• 8	• 7½	• 6	• 5	• 4	• 2	● BB

Comparative sizes of shot.

"Close shots? Who gets 'em?" you ask. Besides, a gun that can hit birds away out yonder should be able to really nail them at a shorter distance. But you've got to consider the human factor. What about *you?*

Let's come clean. Just between you and me, you really don't hit very many of those way-out birds, do you? If that's the case, for most upland shooting your tight-shootin' smokepole is more liability than asset.

Put even more simply, a full choke is for extreme range shooting (beyond forty yards), modified is fine for normal gunning (twenty-five to forty yards), and cylinder for close-range chopping (under twenty-five yards). So, as you may have gathered from the earlier sections, if you hunt only one or two species of birds you may be able to get by with just one gun. But if you hunt all the species discussed you'll need more than one shotgun, or at the least two differently choked, interchangeable barrels for your favorite shot spewer.

If you insist on using only one barrel, say a full-choke, you'll handicap yourself unnecessarily. Much upland shooting is up close, and the small, lightly feathered birds don't kill hard. Just a pellet or two will do it. So you don't need concentration. You want quick, widespread shot dispersion and an even pattern.

Put it this way. Could you knock a beer can off a stump ten yards away more easily with a golf ball or a basketball? Well that's about the comparison between shooting a full-choke and a cylinder boring at most upland game. The open bore's most effective spread is under twenty-five yards, the full's most effective maximum beyond forty.

Even if you're such a crack shot you can hit a small flying bird in close with that little ball of shot a full choke chucks out it still makes no sense. Even if your dog can find and bring back more than the bill and feet, what's in between would be a mashed-up mess.

If these recommendations make sense and you can afford another gun, or a second barrel or set of barrels, keep them in mind when you shop around. The barrel or barrels on an upland gun should not be more than 28 inches long; 26 is much better and you might even like it stubbier. (Remember that the overall length of a double gun will be shorter than a pump or auto because there is no receiver.)

If the new gun or second-barrel route seems too expensive, one of the muzzle devices allowing you to change your gun's choke by the turn of a knob or the insertion of a different tube may strike you as practical. But if, like me, you don't care for that blob on the end of the barrel or your hunting companions' ears are offended by the way the muzzle blast is dispersed, there's still some hope.

Invest in some "spreader" or brush loads when you switch over from pheasant to woodcock or quail shooting. This ingenious little ballistics invention will give you a pretty well-spread pattern even when fired out of a full-choke barrel. The shot in the shell is divided up by wads, and for some reason or another this disperses the shot differently than the single-wadded load does. It won't give you the world's prettiest pattern, but it will increase your chances on small game at close range.

Patterning Your Gun

Now, while choking is done at the factory and the barrel is usually marked designating the degree of choke (either by symbols

ROAD HUNTING

Very few states have regulations prohibiting shooting a game bird while it's on the ground. But most prohibit discharging firearms from a motor vehicle and many require guns being transported in a car to be unloaded and enclosed in a carrying case.

So if you comply with your state's laws it is legal to drive a car down backroads and trails, spot a bird at roadside, stop, get out, load up and ground swat a sitting target. Maybe it's legal but it ain't right.

If you call that "hunting" and fill your bag with "ground sluiced" (pronounced slooshed) birds I wouldn't wish you any bad luck.

But if you happen to break an arm or leg by dismounting from your upholstered internal-combustion steed before it comes to a complete halt; or if it keeps rolling down an incline and into a gulch because you haven't set the brake; or if you ride home in air-conditioned comfort because you ventilated the roof when you loaded prematurely and fired accidentally, don't expect me to shed any tears.

that require some interpretation or by simply stamping "full," "cylinder" or what have you on the barrel), the only way you'll really know how your gun shoots is by "patterning" it.

You may find that your particular shotgun throws either a slightly tighter or slightly more open pattern than the prescribed standard. And it may throw different patterns with different size shot. In fact, some loading companies (and some hand loaders) have learned how to open up or restrict shot patterns by modifying the top wad in the shot shell.

To pattern a gun, tack up a big sheet of wrapping paper, step off forty yards from it, hold on the center of the paper and fire the gun at it. Then pick the approximate center of the heaviest concentration of shot, and using a fifteen-inch piece of string and a pencil, inscribe a thirty-inch circle on the paper. Count the number of pellet holes inside this circle and compare it to the load you fired to get your percentage.

You should repeat this about half a dozen times with each load to get an overall average. For with one shot you may get only 65 per cent inside the circle and with another almost 85 per cent, assuming a full-choked barrel. Also try it with different size shot. Then you'll find out whether the particular barrel you have handles your favorite size as it ought to, or whether you'll have to make some compromises. If the pattern is not relatively uniform (shows a lot of gaping holes) that shot size is not for your barrel.

Gun Fit

Next to choke, the main consideration in selecting a gun is how it fits. Now I know shooters who won't believe a gun can fit them unless it was custom made, or at least custom stocked for them. There are gun dealers who claim the same thing, and are happy to demonstrate it—for a price. I could be wrong, but I think much of that talk is a lot of guff. It seems to me that unless you've got a build like a circus freak, instead of worrying about getting a gun to fit you, you'd be better off practicing fitting yourself to a gun.

Of course, a short man, a woman, or a child will do much better with a gun stocked slightly shorter than the regular issue that comes off the production line, and the fellow with very long arms and neck is going to have a different problem than the man with a bull neck and high cheekbones. But all this gets just a bit too esoteric for me. If you think gun fit is the problem causing you to miss—and you have the money to get fitted—by all means get to an exclusive purveyor of firearms and go through the routine with the drop, pitch, comb height, etc. Or, you can hack away at the stock yourself. But chances are pretty good most of your missing is caused by a lack of shooting ability rather than poor fit. Most good shots can adjust pretty well to any decent gun you hand them. It's not only possible, but perhaps even desirable to more or less fit yourself to a standard stock and learn to shoot that way.

Just remember that for every man out in the field who has had a gun personally fitted for his needs there must be at least a thousand shooters doing all right with a standard-dimension gun right off the production line. Could a lot of them do better with a custom-fitted gun? Perhaps. But is the price worth it?

I really don't mean to make fun of proper gun fit. But do put it in its proper perspective. Throw a gun to your shoulder. If you're a beginner, rest assured that with practice you can learn to shoot with it. If you've shot a lot, you'll know if it comes up right—for you. Sure, we all have preferences. One of the greatest shotguns ever manufactured was the old Winchester Model 12. Yet, I've never been able to throw one up and have it feel right. So I never bought one.

That's why it takes some shopping around to find the right gun. Some gunners naturally take to the handy balance of a side-by-side double or the quick-handling superposed with its single sighting plane. Others prefer the old reliable pump action or the sometimes more temperamental autoloader. If you like guns, the chances are you'll spend enough time at the dealer's gun rack to become familiar with the various models of all of these, and will probably do some swapping around before finally deciding what really suits you best.

Good second-hand shotguns aren't exactly cheap, but you may find a bargain if the price of a new one seems too steep. Most shotguns made in "trap or skeet grade" have ventilated rib barrels and better wood than the "field grade" guns. I happen to like a vent-rib barrel with two beads, but in a field gun the added weight and nuisance in cleaning makes this a moot point—and ribbed barrels cost more.

Probably the most popular shotgun marketed today is the auto-loader. I don't happen to care for them. It's purely a personal preference, since I just seem to get on well with pump guns. My son, who has had an autoloader since his twelfth Christmas, likes and does right well with a Remington M-1100, 12-gauge auto. The man who totes an autoloader or pump can use the same gun on both quail and waterfowl if he buys an extra barrel, using full for ducks and geese or improved cylinder or skeet for the upland species.

One of the strong recommendations for using a double-barreled shotgun in the uplands is that you get a choice of two chokes with each gun, the more open boring for the first shot, the tighter choke for the second. If you don't spend too much time worrying about which barrel is right for the distance at which the bird gets out, this has advantages.

But actually gun style isn't too important. I confess I once bought a Browning Superposed 20-gauge, at least partially because I have on occasion run with a pack of gentlemen woodcock and quail hunters who frown on anything but a double gun. Being classified as a peasant didn't bother me, but I feared being bad-mouthed as a churlish, ignorant knave to boot if I showed up in their company armed with my favorite pump gun.

So I sunk what seemed like a near fortune into this beautiful-handling little weapon with improved-cylinder and modified boring when the going price for the "economy" model was around $300, figuring it would be my Beau Ideal of a bird gun. But either I got a lemon or this model was too delicate for my use. Too many malfunctions soured me. I sold it. (It, along with some of the two-shot autoloaders I shot, led me to jump to the conclusion that Browning chokes its guns tighter than U.S. companies, and the buyer who gets a double for quail, ruffed grouse and woodcock should get the most open bore combination available.)

Pricewise there has always been a considerable disadvantage in acquiring a double. Twin-tube popularity was probably at its lowest ebb going into the 1960s. Nobody seemed to want a double. As a result, not many were manufactured and even fewer were stocked by local merchants. But going into the 1990s, a lot has changed. There has been a resurgence of interest in double-barreled shotguns, mostly manufactured in Japan.

There *is* something about the feel and appearance of a fine double that sets it off. Furthermore the double has always had some snob appeal and it seems that a lot of people today have a little extra wad of money burning holes in the toe of their socks and are investing it in fine equipment. Judging from the most recent trade and sport shows, double barrels are about the hottest thing on the gun market.

New and re-issued models are offered by U. S. and foreign firms. They cost from somewhat to a great deal more than domestic pumps and autoloaders which now offer some light and nifty models well fitted for the uplands, as well as hefty goose-knockers. The last serviceable side by side that was priced in repeater range was Savage Arms' Fox Model B, non-selective single trigger. It proved out okay for me but today's foreign fusils will feel better in the hands of a dedicated gun nut.

Classic U. S. side-by-sides are now available mostly as high-priced second-hand guns. But you can still order new the Model-21 Winchester or reproductions of Parkers. But these babies are too costly and beautiful for brush banging. You'll probably fondle them and shoot them only at trap or skeet or the new sporting clays when they're not on envy-rousing display in your gun cabinet.

In the over-and-under field, still dominated by Browning Arms, you'll find stacked-tube Winchesters, Ithaca-SKBs, Dalys and Remington Model 32s on used gun sales racks. Still available fresh out of the box are two excellent models, as good or better than anything past and present, the Weatherby Orion and the Ruger Red Label. The price for their design, balance, appearance and durability is reasonable. They combine prestigiousness and practicality.

Should you decide on a love affair with any double gun, do it with both eyes open. In my limited experience with these Dresden dolls of the gun world they demand a lot more tender, loving care and attention than does that old reliable housewife, the pump gun, or even the temperamental autoloader. Like me, you may also find yourself reluctant to expose one to the abrasive facts of life that are a part of hard hunting—brush, rain, sand, mud and bumps.

Furthermore, if your double gun has a single trigger which depends upon recoil from the first shot to arm the second barrel, don't get caught off guard, as I have several times in good woodcock cover during a flight. (And a good hunting buddy of mine, had the same thing happen to him while we were on a sharptail shoot in Saskatchewan. So it isn't just me.)

What happens is you get off one shot at a single bird. Hit or miss, you hold up a minute, then "break" the gun to reload. But just as you reach for that shell, another bird or birds get up. You snap the gun shut, mount it and mentally count a dead bird in the bag as you swing through. Only thing wrong with the whole show is that opening the gun automatically recocked the first barrel, so that the firing pin clicks on an empty chamber. That's bad enough. But you can jerk the trigger again right to the back of the trigger guard and the second barrel will do you no good since there was no recoil to recock the trigger.

I know, I know, an autoloader can get gummed up or freeze in cold weather and you can even "short-shuck" a pump when you're excited. But those have to do with maintenance and human malfunction rather than design or mechanical malfunction. You can't honestly cuss out a gun for that.

9
Wardrobe For The Uplands

IF it's comfortable, it's right for you. That's about the only cut-and-dried rule about upland game hunting clothing a serious hunter has to remember.

This land of ours is so large that many different weather and terrain conditions exist under which the same bird species can be hunted. Any generalized statements about hunting clothing will have to allow for so many exceptions that it might be questioned if there are any rules to follow.

There is at least one more general axiom: If you find something in the line of hunting clothing that just suits you and is practical and durable, buy two or three, or more, right now! For manufacturers of hunting gear have shown a distressing tendency to junk almost anything that's really useful and replace it with something that must have been designed by a maiden aunt whose knowledge of the needs and anatomy of a hunter were purely guesswork!

But let's have a crack at some recommendations, starting at the bottom. Any avid upland game hunter should have at least three pairs of boots. They should be the all-leather boot, the rubber-bottom, leather-top pac, and a light 12-inch all-rubber boot.

Oil-tanned leather is best in the all-leather boot; it stands up best, bounces back soft after a soaking, and is easily restored by application of a good grade of boot grease. The soles should be crepe or a rubber-type composition. The boots should have heels.

The sharp edges of a heel may save you a nasty spill and will not cause slipping the way a wedge sole can.

Soles and heels should not be too hard. If an outfit guarantees some soles to outlast the uppers, forget those boots. They'll wear like iron but will be like walking on horseshoes. You'll get tired legs and even headaches from a pounding that softer soles could absorb. Furthermore, they are criminally slippery.

This boot should lace. Whether by eyelets, hooks or the new, so-called "speed lacer" eye-hook arrangement is immaterial. But a boot that is not laced will slip around on your foot, and the open tops will collect weed seeds, chaff and other debris. Some hunters may prefer simply a high work shoe. But this gives less ankle support, loads up with debris and is no protection against insects, brush scratches, etc.

Walking the uplands will keep feet warm, so shy off of insulated leather boots. Boots invariably get wet, the insulated ones are pains to dry out and are bulky. Leather linings or double vamps are fine, minimal height should be nine inches and twelve is better, protecting without binding; the popular six to eight inch hiker's boots are not hunting footgear.

For my money the rubber-bottom, leather-top boot is the best all-around hunting shoe a man can invest in. However, they are rough on wool socks. (You can save on this if you wear a pair of cotton work socks, commonly called Rockford socks, over those expensive wool jobs.)

This popular pac is great in the early morning hours when there's still frost or dew on the ground, or anywhere where the under-footing is damp, slushy or snow covered. But they can be worn through the dry part of the day as well if it's not too hot, and if you step lively, you can ford shallow creeks without getting your feet wet. In any event, wherever moisture is going to be a problem they beat the all-leather boot. Take them off when you get in the car or come in the house. The rubber can give you clammy feet when you aren't walking.

There are probably a number of different brands on the market that are satisfactory, but I haven't tried most of them because I've been so satisfied with the L. L. Bean model. These rubber-bottom boots are light, comfortable, durable and practical. That's all I can ask in an upland boot.

The all-rubber boot coming halfway up the calf is for very wet conditions. (You might also consider wearing it in the early morning when it's wet, then switching to leather for the remainder of the day. Changing boots and socks at midday is a worthwhile stunt.) You can wade creeks and puddles with these boots but it's easy to slop over the tops. Then too, rubber doesn't "work out dry" like leather. If you're a really serious pheasant hunter you'll also have a pair of hip boots for getting back to those hide-outs in the marshes.

The worst thing you can have is any pair of boots that are too tight. Your feet will expand when you walk all day. So while I don't go along with the idea of getting boots a half-size or so larger than your most comfortable shoes, you *should* consider getting additional width. (If your shoe width is D, try an E for boot width.) Almost as bad as too-small is the too-large boot that slops around on your foot. A good pair of boots should fit like a shooting glove.

So don't buy leather boots too big with the idea of stuffing them with lots of heavy socks. This just doesn't go—you carry more weight around than is necessary, and heat up your feet. In leather boots one pair of heavy boot socks is plenty. In fact, until it gets real cold, I like the white sweat socks, such as basketball players wear, inside my leather boots. In the rubber and rubber-bottom boots a pair of cotton socks over wool has been suggested and the fit in these boots is not as critical as in leather.

I happen to like to do most of my hunting in long underwear, partly for warmth and comfort, but also to save my legs from a lot of chafing and nicks. This is in temperatures below 55 or 60 degrees; when it gets hot, long underwear is needlessly heavy and heating. The two-piece suit allows you to remove the top part if the day starts out brisk but warms up by mid-morning. You don't need wool—cotton underwear is fine. The moving about will keep you warm. However, I do like wool tops and cotton bottoms for wool soaks up sweat and withstands rain, and doesn't get clammy cold when wet.

As to the outer clothing, you'll see hunters in everything from bib-overalls to some fancy-trimmed outfits that look real good on the mannikins in the store windows but cause snickers in the woods.

But don't judge a man by what he wears. I recall being asked to guide a fellow on a pheasant hunt who showed up clad the way that I imagine a British squire would consider fashionable—Sherlock Holmes hat and all.

On the very first bird, one of my Labradors took down a corn row and pushed the running rooster into the air. I cussed at the dog as I lowered my gun because the bird was too far out to even think of shooting. That's when I heard that imported Austrian side-by-side boom on my right. That long bird collapsed stone dead. "Everybody can get lucky," thought I. But the guy kept on doing it for the rest of the day. The only shot he missed was one coming right over his head, and I blame that on the tight choke of his barrels.

On the other hand, that farmer in the bib-overalls is no object for scorn either. Long ago these agricultural gentlemen discovered what an active man is comfortable in. Those loose overalls, supported by suspenders with no belt cutting a man's middle, are comfortable. They are much more practical than the stylish, but binding, hunting pants that are retailed through most of the sporting goods stores.

There is only one reason for tucking pants cuffs into boot tops: to conserve heat and help keep warm. Seldom does an upland hunter need to do this. That's why the bird hunter who runs around with his pants tucked into his boots is immediately classified as little more an an avid reader of sporting catalogs where all the models are posed with tucked-in pants.

Pants cuffs should swing free to allow unrestricted movement. Furthermore, if the going gets wet and pants are tucked in, the water runs down inside a boot instead of outside and wool sock tops serve as collectors of burrs and other woods and field debris. Even the zouave-style hunting pants with a tight wool cuff, designed for tucking in, might be better utilized outside the boot than in.

I like double-faced pants for bird hunting, whether the extra leg-fronts are just extra material, leather, Naugahyde or nylon. They should have wide belt loops, suspender buttons, a wide enough cuff so the leg swings free, and the extra facing hung high enough on the pants so I don't have to fight it every time I lift my leg. Hip pockets should have button-down flaps.

Avoid pants with cuffs so narrow they have to be unzipped before

TABLE BIRDS

If it's recipes you're looking for you're out of luck . . . this is no cook book. If you weren't fortunate enough to marry a good cook, there's no help for you here. Outside of some crude camp fire ministrations I've never cooked a game bird.

It sure would be nice if every mother would teach her daughters how to clean and cook game birds. Then us providers of the provender could stomp into the house, skid the birds across the kitchen floor, stretch out in an easy chair with a stiff belt of bourbon in one hand and a tired dog's ear in the other and forget about those damn birds until opening hour next morning.

Hopefully today's liberated women are also "sportspersons" and will give male chauvinist quarry like me a sporting chance to take wing before shooting us down. But any person who runs for President on a platform which provides federal funds to teach all brides to dress game and cook it and then sets up an enforcement agency to see that the techniques are carried out - by the ladies - gets my vote. Every practitioner of the honorable profession of upland bird hunting would be in hog heaven if he had a helpmate who plucks and guts birds.

you can get your foot in, and see that the manufacturer had sense enough to put the suspender buttons on the outside, where they won't gall you. Forget about pants with belt loops so narrow that you can hardly shove even a rope through them. Hunting pants should be "stagged off" short, so they just clear your boot tops. So it makes you look a little "Dutchy," not slim and trim like the advertisements, but it will pay off in comfort and safety.

Blue-jeans? Fine, if you're riding around, either on a horse or in an automobile. But made for all-day walking, they ain't.

Wear any shirt that's comfortable. For my part this usually means wool, although cotton flannel worn over a wool shirt will keep it clean and won't pick up as many sticktights. In warm climates the long-sleeved cotton work shirts are the answer. Every hunting shirt should have flap pockets that button, and should button all the way up the front. Then it can be snugged up at the neck to conserve heat, or opened up to let out the steam when you get sweated up. Avoid clinging or tight-necked sweaters and sweat shirts.

The so-called hunting coats that millions of hunters invest in are abominable. They are heavy, binding, too hot in warm weather and give little warmth for the weight in cold weather.

The outermost garment an upland hunter wears should provide a place to carry his shells and the birds he shoots, and also have pockets for such things as sandwiches, gloves, smoking materials and other minutiae.

The vest is the answer to this. Furthermore it can be worn over the lightest or heaviest clothing. If it's raining, it can be worn over rain gear. It's light, and there is a freedom of action with one's arms unencumbered. At the same time, when buttoned or zipped up it provides a windbreak for the body when a chill wind is blowing.

However, avoid those vests that provide for toting your shot shells in elastic loops spread all over the front of the vest. You'll lose a fortune in shells because every time you bend over, your ammunition will pop out of these loops and fall on the ground. There is only one place for these loops—inside the two big pockets on each side of the vest, pockets with a flap over them.

Look also for a roomy game pocket and one with generous openings. Most upland hunting vests seem designed for the quail hunter only, and you can hardly cram a pheasant through the skimpy access slots to the game pocket. The best bird vest I've discovered so far has a convenient opening in the front which lets you stuff a bird in without laying gun down and twisting your arm off to get it in the back slot.

For shooting in really cold weather, the garment to be worn over the wool shirt and under the hunting vest should be one of the nylon-shell types, filled with synthetic insulation. Properly designed it allows plenty of free swinging and is light and warm.

Hats are a matter of choice. They can range from everything just short of a Mexican sombrero to a baseball player's cap. Primarily, they should provide shade for the eyes and face, and protection for the eyes against twigs and brush. A long-billed or broad-brimmed hat does this. I mostly use a duck-hunter's hat, with some brim; they're light and comfortable, and can be turned inside out to give a dog a drink. You might consider a bright color instead of camouflage so your hunting buddies can spot you more readily in thick cover.

Some hunters can shooting wearing gloves. If you can, fine. Wear light ones to protect your hands against scratches or heavier ones to keep warm. But I can't shoot with a glove on my trigger finger, so I solve the problem in cold weather by wearing a glove on my left hand and keeping the bare right hand frequently in my pants or jacket pocket. Works pretty good.

Every man who hunts hard should have a good pair of shooting glasses—and wear them. They are cheap protection for the eyes from sun glare, twigs and projectiles, and amber lenses can sharpen things up on murky days. If you're like me you'll sometimes forget to take them along, but you ought to own them, anyway.

The upland bird hunter will find many uses for a good jackknife in his pocket and a small sheath-knife on his belt. The boy scout type jackknife with blade, screwdriver, awl, bottle- and can-opener is most practical. A sharp, slim, sheath knife with a four- or five-inch blade will be handy for field dressing and dismembering birds or slicing the breakfast bacon.

That's a rough outline of what's proven practical for me. If you prefer to carry your shells in a belt (and don't mind looking like Pancho Villa) or like a game bag better than a vest, go right ahead. For as I said at the beginning of this book, upland bird hunting is the most diversified and democratic of all the hunting sports; there is no uniform mode of hunting, and certainly no specific hunting uniform. You don't have to be ashamed of anything you wear when upland bird hunting, even your oldest pair of pants and a tattered shirt. For you'll have lots of company; lots of men who can afford special hunting clothing think it's a waste of money, or prefer clothing that's been hanging on the edge of the rag bag.

So deck yourself out in whatever is comfortable and practical for you, and have at it. Nobody will sneer at battered, well-worn but action-allowing clothes, but many hunters will look askance at a stylish dude who moves as if he's wrapped up in a straightjacket!

10
Gun Dogs
For The Uplands

A WELL-trained or even a partially broke dog can provide so much more hunting and add so much to the pleasure of a day in the field that it's hard to imagine a valid reason for not using a canine of some sort to hunt with.

Sure, I admit to prejudice along those lines. I suppose I understand why someone who has had an unfortunate experience with a poorly trained or natural sad sack of a dog might say, "No thank you, Mac. I'd rather do it myself." I realize that others may figure a dog is too much bother, or argue that they can't afford it. Perhaps it's true that a dog can be a lot of bother, but the hunter who "can't afford" a dog is nothing more than an excuse-maker—he usually affords a lot of other things that give him less enjoyment than a halfway decent hunting dog would.

As for the man whose wife won't let him have a dog, one can only feel sorrow, for when that happens—*well!* But let me say this—the ladies of this world, bless their souls, are like good poker players. If they've held the upper hand too long, they sure learn how to bluff. Years ago my dearly beloved laid down the law in no uncertain terms. (It's not that she hates dogs. She just doesn't think they're cheaper by the dozen.) Quoth she, "You bring one more dog home and I leave." That was, by most recent count, some 27 dogs ago and she's still around. Of course, I don't know *your* wife.

With that out of the way, let's get down to some off-the-cuff opinions about dogs, some advice about what's going to be best for the hunting you do, and so forth. This is not a treatise on dog training. If you want to train a gun dog—pointer, spaniel or retriever—I heartily recommend *Hunting Dog Know-How* by one David Michael Duffey, published by Winchester Press. I agree with everything it says.

But let me try to lay out some guidelines, to aid you in your selection of a dog or perhaps give you a bit of insight into why the dog you already own behaves as he does. Just remember, I'm not in the business of promoting any specific kind of dog. I admire any dog, of any breed, who does the job he's supposed to the way it's supposed to be done.

As a hunter you have a wide choice. Our more popular hunting breeds are also good prospects as family pets, companions and children's playmates. And, contrary to some expressed opinions, they can't get too much human attention. Playing with the kids is good for a dog, and the more you have him with you and the family, the better dog he'll be.

There are three broad classifications of dogs that can be used on upland game: pointing dogs, spaniels and retrievers. Each group has a specialty, but individual dogs from individual breeds within each group can be developed into multi-purpose dogs, if they are intelligent and are given opportunities on the game you want to hunt. Much of the secret of training a dog lies with giving the dog a chance to do what his instincts and desire to please you will lead him to doing.

For quail, you will want a pointing dog—a dog that will range out, find game, point it and remain pointing, until you approach, walk in and flush it. When working this kind of dog, the man does the flushing. (Pointing dogs which bump up quail are next to worthless because if they have enough range to be worth feeding, they will usually be out beyond gun range.)

The English Setter and Pointer are the two breeds leading the list here, but you may find yourself the proud owner of a good Irish or Gordon Setter that can do the job. The on-foot quail hunter may also find one of the Continental breeds (Brittany Spaniel, German Wirehaired Pointer, German Shorthaired Pointer, Vizsla or Weimaraner) just the ticket.

Sure, you can use a spaniel or retriever to hunt quail. I've mentioned previously that I've used them under certain conditions. But quail are for pointing dogs.

Pheasants, on the other hand, are the spaniel's dish of tea. (Some of the retrievers—Labrador, Golden, Chesapeake or Irish Water Spaniel—trained to work in the manner of the spaniel can also be top pheasant-rousters.) The spaniel's manner of hunting is to bustle about, quartering the ground within gun range of the hunter, scenting and then driving in to put the bird into the air. You can pick from English Springer Spaniels, American Water Spaniels, Boykin Spaniels, or English Working Cocker Spaniels.

When it comes to ruffed grouse, the traditional dog has long been the grouse-trained English Setter. If you insist on using a pointing dog on these spooky birds and are buying a pup, the Brittany can be favored on percentages. Because the cover is thick, a close-working pointing dog is preferred. Most Britts are just that. The other Continental breeds can also fill the bill, as can a properly broke Pointer, Irish or Gordon Setter. (When you acquire a trained dog, forget about breed; just get a dog that does it the way you want it done. But puppies are gambles, and I'm suggesting best bets.)

However, I think you'll probably have more fun and get more birds if you work ruffed grouse with a flushing dog. The spaniels excel at this. The retrievers can adapt to it. You can see your dog and know what he's doing practically all the time. With a pointing dog you must often try to find your dog in impossibly thick cover and you hestitate to call him when he's gone for fear he may be on point. Beepers and bells aid in locating moving and stationary dogs.

About the same things can be said in regard to recommendations for a woodcock dog, except that the woodcock holds well for a pointing dog. The ruffed grouse does not and that's what makes it a most difficult bird for a pointing dog to handle. Grouse hunters who use pointing dogs more often than not find themselves shooting over flushes or stops-to-flush rather than a good solid point. This is not true of the woodcock. If you can find your dog on point in the thick stuff, rest assured that the woodcock will be there.

But on woodcock the flushing dog still gets the nod. He can be sent down into the thick stuff to roust out the birds while you stay out in the clear as much as possible. With a dog on point you must go to the dog, and that means being down in the thickets where vision and gun swing are hampered.

Just a note about woodcock. Many an otherwise fine retriever just won't pick up these little rascals. Try your best to get your dog to fetch them. But if he refuses don't push to the point where he becomes reluctant to do any retrieving.

Because they like wide-open country the Hungarian partridge and prairie grouse are best hunted by a pointing dog, and a wide-ranging one at that. The work is similar to that done on quail. But if in addition to being a good bobwhite dog, the Pointer or Setter has proved himself able to handle pheasants, he'll probably make a crackerjack Chicken, Sharptail and Hun hunter.

But you want a dog that will do everything? An all-purpose dog? There ain't no such breed, but there are individual animals within all the breeds that will master a multiplicity of duties. As a rule, however, they will handle one or two species better than the others. And if you make a trip to hunt some game strange to your dog, allow him a day or two to get accustomed to it and find out what you want and how this new bird is to be handled.

Maybe you are in country where there are several varieties of game. You're likely to run across a sampling of everything that's legal and you want a dog that can handle it all. The English call this "rough shooting."

An upland game hunting buddy, Bob Distin, and I enjoyed just such a shoot a few falls back, all within a ten-mile radius of my home. In the course of the day we had shooting at ruffed grouse, woodcock, pheasant, duck, Hungarian, Jacksnipe, squirrel and rabbit.

Bob still chuckles about how we crowded in every minute possible in a long hunting day. There were ten minutes of shooting time left when we passed a man whose car had slid off the road and into a ditch. I stopped long enough to tell him we'd be back in about twenty minutes and pull him out. With five minutes of shooting time left we reached the little corn patch I was aiming for and got into the feeding Hungarians. Then we went back and pulled the car back on the road. The driver was grateful, but I'm sure he thought we were nuts. But then, aren't all hunters?

For this kind of catch-as-catch-can hunting nothing beats a spaniel, or any flushing dog taught to hunt in this manner. You

FEE HUNTING

Free hunting has long been a thing of the past in the U.S. although sportsmen grumble about its passing and resent having to pay for the privilege while willingly shelling out for greens fees at the country club or tickets on the 50-yard line.

All hunting today is fee hunting, whether payment is made for state and federal licenses or stamps, leasing hunting rights on private land or commercially managed hunting area where birds are propagated and stocked for the gun.

In common with racehorses, bird dogs and women, there are good, bad and indifferent commercial hunting set-ups. If you are a hunter, enjoy good dog work and sporty shooting but can't find enough open land or enough birds on it to satisfy your yen, by all means locate a well-run hunting club and pay your fee. It will pay off for you.

Enjoy the opportunity to fully train your dog and sharpen your wing-shooting skills on the real thing without apology. Chances are the self-professed "wild bird" hunter whose macho image of himself wouldn't allow him to patronize a gun club is a member of the crew that synchronizes its visits to public hunting grounds with the arrival of the state truck from which pheasants are thrown out to insure John Q. Hunter gets a return for his license fee. You pay your own way, don't deplete wild game populations and don't pretend to be something you ain't. Done right, on the right place and it's damn good hunting.

will also find spaniels and retrievers to be surer in the recovery of downed game than pointing dogs, as a rule.

Now if you lean toward waterfowl hunting, by all means stick with the Labs, Goldens and Chessies, and accept what they can do for you in the uplands. If conditions are not too severe, the spaniels can also double as duck-fetchers and you will probably see more German Wirehairs and Shorthairs and Brittany spaniels doing a little duck fetching, if their masters gun aquatic game only occasionally, than you'll find Pointers or Setters doing this job.

A rule of thumb to follow is this: If the country is big and relatively open, rely on a pointing dog to find you more birds and save you a lot of unnecessary walking. But if the areas are small and the cover is dense or thick enough so that it must be carefully hunted, the flushing dog will put more game in your bag. This will hold true regardless of the game species hunted because in different parts of the country the same game bird may frequent different type cover.

Should you enjoy rabbit or maybe squirrel hunting along with your upland bird shooting, there's no reason a Beagle or a Basset hound may not work out for you. Plenty of these hounds are used to produce pheasants and ruffed grouse and their owners are well satisfied with them.

A friend of mine down in Dodge county, Bill Stark, had a pair of little cur dogs whose pushed-in faces and undershot jaws bespoke their Boston terrier ancestry. It was always a source of great joy to him when they held their own or topped the work of my favorite Labradors when it came to pushing pheasants out of thick marsh cover.

Milo Mabie's best woodcock dog was a cross between Weimaraner and Labrador. Working with a cowbell on his collar he stayed within gun range and within seconds after the bell stopped jangling, Milo would be on the alert for a woodcock to chitter to the top of the cover. For although the dog was often screened from sight by the dense cover, he'd flash-point long enough to stop the bell, then jump in and flush.

So even if you own something that's off-beat or a mongrel, give the dog a chance. The main thing is to get a dog and use him. If he doesn't learn, or is hopeless, start over with one of the breeds mentioned here that best fits your situation, follow the training procedure outlined in a good book on the subject and watch your success ratio climb.

Furthermore, you'll be able to lay claim to being a conscientious conservationist as well. For few will be the downed birds that a good dog will not recover.

CHECK LIST OF BREEDS AVAILABLE TO THE HUNTER

Retrievers: Labrador, Golden, Chesapeake Bay, Curly-Coated, Flat-Coated, Irish Water Spaniel.
Spaniels: English Springer, American Water, Boykin, English Cocker, Cocker, Welsh Springer, Sussex, Field and Clumber.
Pointers: Pointer, English Setter, Irish Setter, Gordon Setter, German Wirehaired Pointer, German Shorthaired Pointer, Vizsla, Weimaraner, Brittany Spaniel, Pudelpointer, Wirehaired Pointing Griffon.

11
Hunting Tactics

Bird Hunting Weather

LIKE many writers, the gentleman who wrote the song "Isn't It A Lovely Day To Be Caught In The Rain" probably wasn't much of a practitioner of what he preached. In other words, he didn't have to be out in the wet stuff much.

There is nothing more miserable than chasing girls or hunting game birds in a downpour. And seldom is it productive. But a little rain ain't bad and a drizzly day can be right good as far as bird hunting goes. In fact, the only days when I would advise a hunter to forget the whole bit and stay home are days that feature a strong wind.

So "let's look at the weather picture," as the TV prognosticator says, before proceeding to further confuse what the weather bureau has already mucked up. The only really intelligent thing I can say about the weather *and prove* is that there isn't much you and I can do about it. We just have to live with it. Our society being what it is, a man can't hunt according to the weather. When he schedules a hunting day, that's the day he's got to go, rain, shine and everything in between.

In a way, this works out all right. If you start trying to set up your hunting trips according to what somebody tells you the weather is going to be you just won't take many. I don't mean you should tune off the weather report and go to bed the night before a day in the field; it's nice to anticipate what may happen on the morrow. Just don't lose sleep over it.

As mentioned, if you wake up that fine morning and the wind is howling, roll over and forget about bird hunting. All game is spooky in a wind and upland birds probably more so than any other. Furthermore, hearing is a definite aid to an upland bird hunter, since your first inkling of a bird's presence may be the noise made when he rushes into flight. During a wind, not only will the birds sneak up farther out than normal but you won't hear them. This may lead you to the conclusion that there are no birds in this particular bit of cover. It may cost you a fine hunt on another day.

I'd rate steady rain as the second-worst kind of weather for upland bird hunting, particularly cold rain, sleet or snow. The reason for this, to me at least, is simple as can be. It's plain uncomfortable, for boy, beast or bird. Birds don't like to move around in this stuff any more than the boys-at-heart who pursue them with shotguns, and many an otherwise fine dog is a poor mudder. So birds sit tight, giving off no scent encouragement to pep up a canine, dogs dog it and men don't make the effort to get with it, and enthusiasm is a prime requirement of really successful hunting.

But if you haven't been caught out in a hard rain you are not much of a bird hunter. For very often some of your best hunting will come just before the storm breaks. Birds have a built-in barometer and they tend to get out and feed up heavily before bad weather moves in. You'll be better off to try to guess what the morrow's weather will be by observing bird activity in the uplands than in scheduling your trips according to predictions about weather.

Overcast days usually provide fine hunting. Birds stay out and move about later in the morning and come out again earlier in the evening. Bitter cold, which can come unexpectedly during northern hunting seasons, ranks up along with windy or downpour days as poor hunting time. Birds sit tight, conserving body heat.

But if you are out with me on a day that's cold, we'll be down in the thick stuff or—late in the season—among the poplar trees where birds bud. And if it's raining hard we'll be looking for some spruce, cedar, balsam, pine or other conifer stands, either dense or sparsely scattered in among the hardwoods or poplar. Birds like to sit tight under this type of shelter.

Much as I usually advocate using a dog, in the winter if one encounters a salt or sugar-snow condition, or crusted snow, a dog will cut down your chances of success. When the snow is grainy it does not hold scent, and a dog is of little use. The noise he makes out in front of you will only chase up birds out of range.

Hunting Partners

A good hunting partner is a gem, a man to cherish. But they are often hard to find. A hunter should be as fussy about the man or men he hunts with as he is about the woman or women he goes to bed with. If you've got no taste, style or pride you deserve just what you get.

So if he's a good man to be in the field with, overlook the minor faults all of us have. If your wife and his don't get along, that's just too bad. Ignore the ladies, stick with the good hunting partner.

Now a man may be lucky enough to have several good hunting buddies. But they should be enjoyed one at a time. Don't hunt in groups or parties. Particularly don't hunt three men to a group. More hunting trips have been ruined by the odd man feeling picked on or left out than for any other cause.

If you must have company, take three other friends along. Then you can split up in pairs and nobody will be left out. And if decisions are to be made, no guy worth hunting with is going to feel put out if he's outvoted three to one. Anything over four in a hunting party is more like a convention, and wives can't be blamed if they become suspicious of your activities.

Spare Gear

During the hunting season, the car of the hunter should at all times contain some kind of a zippered duffle bag or some other carrier to keep necessary and spare gear all in one place and handy.

Included in the pack should be not only dry socks and extra boots, but a complete change of clothing. You can get drenched in a rain or fall off a log crossing a creek. Dry clothing will encourage you to go back hunting even if it doesn't really have an effect on whether you catch cold or not.

Some extra shotgun shells should always be handy and some kind of canned meat and crackers can provide a welcome snack if you decide to stay out through mealtime on the spur of the moment. A suit of coveralls may be the handiest thing to slip into if you find you have a few minutes' time to hunt between appointments or spot some game as you are driving to work.

Be sure that bag contains some rain gear. Parkas are fine but rainsuits (coat and pants) are even better. If your bag is always packed, you can sleep a few minutes later in the mornings you plan to hunt, jump in the car and know when you reach your destination everything you need will be available.

A spare gun also has its place in a hunter's car. Today's firearms aren't prone to break down, but when it happens you're usually a long way from a gunsmith. It might not be as much fun hunting with the "reserve" gun, but any gun is better than none at all and the ruination of a weekend trip or the loss of time to go back home or into town when you've only a few hours to hunt.

Hunt with a Purpose

When you head out on a hunting trip, don't go with the idea of "Oh! I'm not looking for anything in particular. I'll take whatever I run across."

This is a pretty sure way to shoot nothing.

Every trip should be made for a certain species of bird, except in the case where two species may frequent the same terrain, like ruffed grouse and woodcock or prairie grouse and Hungarians. Plans should be geared for one bird.

Hunt specific cover that you think will produce the game bird you've settled on for that morning or that trip. If you want to switch later in the day, okay. But have your gun, load and dog—and most of all your own mind—focused on a particular species.

If you're surprised when something you aren't hunting jumps out, like a pheasant in grouse cover or a duck along a woodcock stream, fine. Shoot it. But recognize it as a bonus and keep your eye on the doughnut, not the hole.

GETTING LOST

Daniel Boone, 'tis said, never got lost. He did, however, confess to getting "turned around" upon occassion, sometimes for two or three weeks at a time.

Maybe you do too. But you are free to create your own myths and excuses about your innate sense of direction. I can't. Too many people are overly willing to testify about how mixed up I can get.

Like the time two clients and I emerged from the brush onto a tote road at dusk finishing a successful woodcock and ruffed grouse hunt in Price County. They apparently concluded that any guide who could find all those little birds ought to be able to locate a full-sized motor vehicle parked off a town road. So they let me argue them into going right up the tote road instead of down it to the left, ignoring a warning from a game warden friend of mine, Buck Urquhart: "This guy's dogs will find you some birds. But he couldn't lead a pack of boy scouts to a candy store. If there's some doubt about which way to go, strike out in the opposite direction to the one he picks and you'll probably come out right."

That evening we had to retrace our steps more than a mile and a half, and hike another mile before reaching the vehicle long after dark! When Urquhart retired and went on the road selling St. Croix fishing tackle I suspect he inspired one Texas gentleman to send me a string tie, with built-in compass, in case I ever hunted in a "big state like Texas."

My advice is buy a compass. Learn to use it. Take it with you. Use it. And when you go hunting always tell someone where you are going and what time you expect to get back.

But all that behind us, let's say the alarm clock has seen to it that you're at your favorite hunting ground a bit before the first crack of dawn and you've seen frost in the glow of your car's headlights.

Never heard of a hunter getting out too early? Chances are good that's just what happened to you. But when the sun comes up and the frost sparkles on the cover, you might as well start hiking as stand around and shiver. I've done this over and over and probably will never learn. I just can't get out hunting early enough. But the fact is that usually about all I shoot during that first hour or so is a few woodcock, if the freeze hasn't been hard enough to move out the residents.

It's not a hard, fast rule. But if you are an on-foot hunter who uses a dog, early on a frosty morning might be a great time to be in Dixie, but it ain't much for partridge hunting in Yankeeland. While it is a well-proven fact that birds move out into the road edges and openings early in the morning, the hunter with a dog will do better if he gives them an hour or so to move around, picking greens and grit, drying off after a long cold night on the roost. About 8 A.M. is a good time to seriously start partridge hunting.

If you are a "road hunter" who uses a motor vehicle to get you to where the birds are, driving slowly down backroads and logging trails until you spot a bird on the road edge, then you'd better get up early. By 8:30 to 9 A.M. (sun time) most of the birds will have moved back into cover at least a little ways, and cannot be produced by your mode of hunting.

Assuming, however, that you are out with me, we'll hike those roads and trails, or work the edges of clearings 'til maybe about 10 A.M. The dogs will pick up scent left by the birds who came out into the trails or along the edges and work back and flush them for shots. It will pay us to make little swings off the road into likely looking spots. But guide off that road or circle the edge of the clearings and fields.

When walking down the two ruts that often serve as a road or path in logging country, a pair of hunters should work out a system.

When a dog starts making game the shooter in the rut nearest the trailside where the dog is working should lag back and the shooter in the rut farthest from the dog move up ahead. Then both will have a chance for a shot when the bird flushes, virtually regardless of its flight direction, without interfering with or endangering each other. Longtime hunting partners do this without thinking. Beginners have to be told.

When following the dogs out into the cover off the trailside, or taking them in to investigate likely spots, if two hunters are going to stay within sight of each other only one should leave the trail at a time. If the off-trail man misses a shot at a flushed bird it's likely that the man on the road will get a relatively open shot if the bird goes back across. The man on the road will also serve as a beacon. Woods trails twist and turn to go nowhere and are easy to lose.

By mid-morning we'll head for the "outback." There is a two-fold reason for waiting until that time of day to hit the brush. First of all, the birds aren't going to be in the thick stuff early in the morning—unless you get out real early on an overcast morning and nail them before they start out for the openings. Secondly, it's pretty uncomfortable hiking through heavy brush before the dew or frost, depending on the place and clime, has been burned off by the sun or sloughed off by a breeze. Only your feet get wet out on a trail or along a clearing. You can get soaked from boots to hat in the brush.

The middle of the day will find us hunting the thick stuff, creek bottoms, islands surrounded by marsh, thickets and overgrown tangles, pine plantations, logged-off ridges running between timber and water (often a good early bet as well, because logging roads follow ridges); any place men are unlikely to be and birds can find refuge after feeding, dusting and sunning.

We may hunt right through midday. But if we've got a cook kit in the car, we may head back to it and make a leisurely and satisfying meal, killing a couple hours eating, napping, fondling our dogs and just enjoying the "vintage wine" that a clear, sunny October day is.

We won't really be idling. We'll be recharging our batteries. It really wasn't too many years ago that I was too impatient to do this. Desire to hunt drove me and almost literally on the run I munched apples, candy bars and battered sandwiches dredged out of my coat pockets.

But the cast iron stomach and the resilient sinews of the very young are no longer mine. So while I'll still pit my ability to hike heavy cover all day when necessary against most challengers, I've learned, like a bird dog past his prime, to husband my energy and actually savor the time spent doing it.

The hours between 11 A.M. and 3 P.M., (give or take an hour either way depending upon various conditions) are the ones in which to relax and catch up on rest if you are on a hunt-every-day schedule, or a trip on which you must make the optimum use of your time but find that early rising and late bedding are sapping your energy.

We might also use the middle of the day to investigate some hitherto unexplored hunting country, either on foot or in a vehicle, as hunting time is precious and you'll probably find me restless after an hour or two of laying up. The point is that too many of today's hunters get out late and quit early. It's a major reason why they don't see and kill more birds.

Game moves morning and evening, but sits tight during the middle of the day. Morning and evening scenting is better for dogs, partially because of the movement of game, but also because of the change in temperature that rising and setting suns provide. Hunters themselves show more ambition at the beginning of a day when they are fresh, or late when they get their second wind, than during the lazy time.

So we'll probably lay up about noon and be back pounding the brush by about 2 P.M. Now we reverse the procedure of the morning. We gradually work our way out of the thick stuff and get back to the edges of the roads and clearings. We'll hunt hard until legal quitting time, which in most states is around dusk. Shoot for as long as the time allows, for some of your best hunting will come just at quitting time. You may well encounter more game in the last half hour of hunting than during most of the rest of the day.

Only a fool is already back at his car and casing his gun when the curtain descends on that day's hunt, unless he already has filled out. Of course, the man who hunts right to the last minute and then reaches his car after dark may well be the despair of a game warden who has staked out on a parked car hoping to nab a law breaker. But if you come in with empty gun and he has heard no shots after closing time, you'll win his grudging respect as a man who likes to hunt and knows what he's doing.

So should you have only a short period each day to hunt, try to locate some coverts near enough to your home so you can clean up your work, get to them by 3 to 4 P.M. and treat yourself to some bird hunting. It's a much more relaxing deal than getting out early in the morning, when you must keep glancing at your watch to estimate how long you have before you must start back in order to get to work on time. A walking hunter should not be thus bedeviled.

Estimating Mileage

To fully savor hunting the uplands, the sportsman must walk. Of course, if the situation calls for it, he may straddle a horse and motor vehicles are wonderful for reaching across the barren stretches of non-huntable country to get the hunter to where the game is.

But only when a man has both feet on the ground can he see the tracks where the raccoon came down to the creek to snatch a frog, the newly constructed beaver dam, the well-beaten deer crossing and the neat line of trotting fox tracks. For these, and other things the foot-slogger will see, add seasoning to the already tasty meat provided by the sight of game and the shooting.

Yet, as important as walking is to the upland hunter, too few have any idea how far they have walked during a given time or how long it takes them to hike across a forty or follow a logging trail for a couple of miles.

Mostly, it's fun to be able to gauge accurately how far you've walked. It also adds to the respect accorded you by woodswise veterans who know walking distances are usually exaggerated. For it's a good bet that when a city-based sportsman tells you he's walked one mile or ten, you get the true measure if you cut his estimate in half.

There are also practical reasons for knowing how far you can walk in an hour or two, like being able to meet a hunting partner at a designated spot at the right time, getting back to camp or work on time and knowing about how long it will take to hunt out a given area.

So try out the formula I've worked out over the years and check it against a map and a watch to set your own pace. Your size, physical condition, stride, experience and attitude will all be factors in this game. You can learn your pace, adding to your craft as an outdoorsman, without detracting from your hunting time.

I've found that moving along briskly, on a logging road or other good unimpeded walking surface or following an eager dog, I'll chalk up a mile in about thirty minutes. That's eight miles in four hours of hunting. But if you move steadily, but hunt carefully you'll probably reduce this pace to about five miles in four hours, or about a mile per forty-five minutes. Hunting very carefully with some difficult cover to negotiate on several occasions may take you an hour or over to cover the mile. If you make a few detours seeking out good game pockets you may take two hours to walk a mile point to point, although you've actually covered a lot more ground.

If you're through hunting and are walking out or if you are hurrying to get to some specific spot, figure you'll hike the mile in about twenty minutes. That's twelve miles in four hours. But it's doubtful you'll maintain that pace the full four hours.

What's your overall average in a day of hunting? If you want to be liberal, count a mile per half-hour. Conservatively you should be able to average a mile per hour. For myself I split the difference, figuring about a mile per forty-five minutes, and sometimes manage to show up in time for meals. Through cover about the fastest a man can move and still claim he's hunting—what with stops to shoot, retrieve birds, wait for a dog to work out scent, etc.—is about a mile to every thirty or forty minutes.

Before you start accusing me of being feeble and pokey, I'm six foot one, weigh about 190 pounds, have a heel-to-heel stride that varies fram thirty-three to thirty-six inches. I walk behind dogs daily, in season and out, and my service time was in the infantry.

So I know a column of soldiers at route march makes about two and a half miles per hour and should wind up twenty miles from the starting point in eight hours of marching, including ten minute breaks on the hour. But you and I are hunting now, buddy, not marching, and it's doubtful that at your age and occupation you could keep pace with a 19-year-old combat infantryman.

In spurt walking you may easily cross a forty (quarter-mile) in four minutes or an eighty (half-mile) in eight minutes but it's much less likely you'll cross a section of land (one mile) in fifteen minutes, although you might step off a mile in fifteen minutes along a hard-surfaced road, with no gun or bag full of birds.

So if my figures aren't acceptable get to work compiling your own. In hunting country that's familiar to you, get a detailed map and find out how far a mile is from one known point to another. Hike some tote road or back road cutting through game country that you've measured with your car's odometer or walk across a farmer friend's forty- or eighty-acre pasture. Check your watch when you start and finish. Get in the habit of doing this from time to time in different terrain under different conditions and you'll soon find your own pace.